FINDING LAVENDER

FINDING LAVENDER

Lauren Morrone

NEW DEGREE PRESS

FINDING LAVENDER

ISBN
978-1-63676-867-0 *Paperback*
978-1-63730-175-3 *Kindle Ebook*
978-1-63730-311-5 *Digital Ebook*

For Gizmo, who was the best dog I could have asked for. Love you forever.

CONTENTS

AUTHOR'S NOTE

I was in middle school when the idea for this story came to me. At the time, I felt like I wouldn't even make it to sixteen, let alone to nineteen and writing a book—this book. It's written from the point of view of a teenage girl to showcase a unique representation of anxiety, depression, and PTSD, rather than the romanticized version in a lot of media today. Creating this story from the perspective of a girl had always felt important to me because of how male-dominated stories like this tend to be. I wanted to see someone like myself out there, and I knew others would want the same thing.

Before I was diagnosed with OCD, social and generalized anxiety disorder, and depression, I went on a mental health journey tons of middle-schoolers go through even today. I was one of those "gifted" kids, a part of what seemed like an elite gathering of other people my age who were only the best of our grade, but I had never felt like I fit in with them. My head was often scrambled, it was hard for me to stay focused on tasks, and I could *never* speak to another person without feeling sick.

Since I didn't have access to resources that would help me understand myself and no one spoke about my conditions, it took research for me to find out what anxiety was and why it was an illness. I never felt like I could bring these issues up around friends or even family because no one else seemed be to experiencing anything similar. I was truly alone.

Thoughts of my younger self make me smile now, but in reality, it isn't funny I had no one to tell me there wasn't anything wrong with me. I thought I was lazy because of the debilitating way depression overcame my brain, preventing me from performing everyday tasks. I thought I was slow for not getting things right away in class. I was making excuses when I didn't want to be around others because of the fear and sheer anxiety that consumed me. Really, I just needed help navigating a part of myself I hadn't been aware of.

It's extremely easy to get caught up in believing the worst, as I once did. I thought I was alone, I was crazy. But I'm not alone. No one is alone when it comes to struggling with mental illness and having a mental illness doesn't make me—or you—crazy.

Even so, symptoms for such conditions vary greatly. Some symptoms are nonexistent for one person, whereas they might be a primary worry for another.

Along with feeling like an outsider because of the way my brain worked, it took me nineteen years to come to terms with my identity as a member of the LGBTQ+ community. From day one, I felt like an outcast. I didn't fit in at school, in any extracurricular activities, and found it nearly impossible to form strong friendships. As I continue to get older, I am still learning to understand my identity more and more. But there is something in the way I didn't think being queer was an option for me. Not that it was a decision I was due to make, but I never even knew queer people really existed or I was one of them. For my entire life, a huge aspect of my being was repressed due to a lack of knowledge.

It's embarrassing how little representation of LGBTQ+ youth there is in all media, not just literature. According to GLAAD, in 2018, 55 percent of films had inclusive representation of only gay men. About 55 percent represented lesbians, and only 15 percent represented bisexuals.[1] It's no wonder my journey with sexuality took nineteen years to come to a head, that my childhood felt like a shelter. How is it the nine million people making up the LGBTQ+ community in the US alone cannot find themselves in popular media? Not only that, but why is the only representation glorified and unrealistic?

The effects of this lack of representation are detrimental. Though the research is scarce, according to the American Psychological Association, members of the LGBTQ+ community are three times more likely to have suicidal thoughts and/or tendencies and have higher rates of attempted suicide when compared to cisgender and heterosexual people.[2] And still, we are not giving the community rightful, normalized representation in media and beyond.

Representation matters.

Without this representation, teens are inherently alone from the day they realize they're different. It breaks my heart. I've only just been accepted into the LGBTQ+ community after coming out, after *years* of suppressing what I thought was abnormal because of how little it was discussed or present in the media. It feels like a dream to be where I am right now, and I can only hope others can get to this place, too.

You should not *have* to wait until you're old enough to be in college to accept and understand yourself. Just because this has always been the norm doesn't mean it *should* be. On the contrary, society needs to do better of making LGBTQ+ youth and youth affected by mental illnesses feel included and welcome.

I hope reading this book helps anyone who feels like an outcast in their situation feel less alone. I hope reading this book can take away some of the worries that go along with not totally understanding oneself or one's sexuality or identity. And I hope reading this book can be the friend some may lack in their homes or schools, so someone feels like they *aren't* a freak, like they aren't abnormal, or feeling things they shouldn't feel.

I thought I was entirely alone at thirteen. I was so confused, hurt, and let down by the society I was living in since it didn't seem to accept any part of me. No one else should feel like that.

You are not alone. You are never alone.

CHAPTER ONE

As the car rumbles down the highway, my veins are flooded with anxiety. I'm putting on my best bored face to tell the social worker to my left this is the most chill I have ever been. My heart, however, feels as though it could burst out of my chest. If that happened, at least I wouldn't have to move into another foster home.

The clunky gray sedan hits a bump, making me wince. With my throat tight, eyes cast upward, fists clenched, I know there is not one thing in this world that would ease my mind right now.

My brain tends to shout unreasonable things at me. It likes to pick moments like this, when I'm filled with anxiety and stress, to scream at me to do things like flex my fingers, tap them, or stretch them. And after I do that, I'm told to scrunch my nose, clench my teeth, and clear my throat. It's been this way since the darkness rolled in, and I've never been able to put a stop to it. I've never spoken about it to anyone, either. I keep it to myself so no one thinks I'm more of a freak than I already am. It usually doesn't get to me, but right now, I would kill for my brain to shut up so I can focus on not throwing up on this social worker's dashboard.

As I'm focusing, I notice Jacob has taken his eyes off of the road to give me a questioning glance. His right hand rests on the steering wheel, left elbow on the window frame, hand worrying at his scruffy beard. His pitiful concern no longer fazes me, but it still makes me sigh a little.

Wordlessly, I dare him to break the silence that had settled between us the moment we sat in this car. He has to know I hate talking, especially to him. There is an unspoken tension because of this that simmers in the air between us alongside the car engine and occasional honking. I know sooner or later he will say something.

He chooses sooner.

"You okay?" Jacob asks, his eyes stuck to the road.

I jump even though I predicted it. "Yes." My voice comes out cold, but inside I feel like I'm boiling. Jacob probably turned the heat up when I wasn't paying attention.

"You sound it," Jacob informs me. He's dull, unenthusiastic, but the sarcasm bleeds through anyway. Our tones would be similar if mine didn't have such a bite.

I don't respond, though my mind whirs. I know Jacob but not very well. Even so, it's easy for someone in his position to assume how I'm feeling considering he's done things like this hundreds of times. This is just another job for him, another drop-off. The only difference is this drop-off is a bit farther than usual because Child Protective Services and the nice people who work there figured it was worth it to find somewhere that would actually be good for me. Supposedly, the house I'm on my way to is my *forever home*.

I think that's a load of garbage considering this is my *fifth* forever home, but it is what it is. It's just another stop for me. And it's easy to guess what Child Protective Services thinks is best for me is juvie. I wouldn't be surprised if this actually was the group home with barred windows I've been expecting. But I've been told I'll be spared that environment so long as I keep my behavior under control.

We'll see about that.

My thoughts fade into a gray haze at the back of my mind as my head throbs slightly. It's a gloomy November day, but the light from outside still bothers my sensitive eyes. I decide to focus on the white line painted on the road. It seems to go on forever.

I wonder distantly if *I* will be able to go on forever, or at least for my whole lifetime. That highway line may fade and fade over the years, but there will always be somebody to fix it up, to make it look nice again, maybe even repaint it so it's brand new. Not me. With each move, I feel like I become less and less me. Maybe one day I'll be so full of nothing I'll blow away, and I won't have to worry about the stupid foster care system or a forever home ever again.

"I think you'll like it in Springfield," Jacob says, interrupting my thoughts.

"Okay," is all that I say, because I have nothing else to contribute. Of course, he'd say I'll like this new town. It's basically his job to find someplace I like, but the problem is he—and any other social worker—doesn't *actually* know what any "problem child" really needs. He'd say I don't communicate well enough, which I guess I agree with, but I can't even imagine putting my thoughts about my life into words. When I try, there's just uninterrupted screaming from my brain, which chooses this path consistently, especially when I could use some quiet. Talk about a headache.

"I was told you were more talkative than this." His tone is lighthearted. I know he's trying to break through the barrier that coats my skin so I'll open up to him in some way, but it isn't happening. I learned long ago not to trust anyone in his position.

I don't feel a response is necessary, so I keep all of my attention on the passing greenery. I haven't seen this much in a really long time. I've become so accustomed to the concrete and brick of the city this could almost be exciting. Almost.

"Are you feeling okay?" Jacob asks. I turn to glare at him. Take in the scruffy brown beard and tired eyes. He spares a glance at me and tries his best to smile. But he got up early today, as I did, and his face is much too wan for it to mean anything. "Are you, you know... in any pain?"

At my last foster home, I was involved with some violent students and ended up getting pretty banged up. But that was a few weeks ago, and I've returned to feeling numb since then.

"No," I deadpan. I hope my eyes are shooting daggers at him right now. I don't want to speak. I don't *want* to tell him to shut up, but I will.

He nods slowly. Maybe I've gotten lucky. Maybe he really will give me some peace and quiet so my throbbing headache can begin to subside.

I know I've missed luck when he sighs deeply, then says, "I have some ibuprofen if you need it. I was told you had a concussion and you bruised your—"

"*Please* shut up."

"Excuse me?"

"What?" I shrug, rolling my eyes. "I said please."

Jacob huffs and puffs beside me. He shifts in his seat, adjusting his hold on the steering wheel. The look he gives me is half surprised and half angry. He's never experienced my attitude, clearly. He has a right to be unsettled, but I wish he'd quit it with the sighing already, because the smell of coffee and cigarettes coming off his breath is only making the pain in my head worse. But I'll take the sighing over talking, I suppose. He stops trying to get me to talk after that. The occasional glare in my direction is the extent of our communication for the next hour or so.

My eyes hold contact with my own reflection in the car's side mirror. I take note of the limp blond strands of hair that are overdue for a wash, the purple circles under my eyes that make my skin look even paler than it is. The fact my eyes are so dark don't do much for the pallor but instead make me look like a vampire of some sort. Quickly, I shut my eyes to get this image out of my brain.

I end up falling into a strange sleep at some point, but I'm thrown out of it as Jacob's car hits a pothole and I'm jerked from my seat. Without looking in the social worker's direction I realize we're definitely approaching the house since we've made it into the suburbs. I was told I would be moved into a place like this because of how poorly the city situation worked out for me.

Out my window, I notice a huge field of grass that goes on until it meets a road parallel to the one I'm on now. The field is surrounded by a sparsely populated forest of trees colored with gold, red, and orange. Against the gray of the sky, the trees create a picturesque fall day.

I prefer the gloom rather than the sun. Especially in the fall, when the world is getting ready for Halloween, the clouds fit better. It's comforting no matter where I go, I can count on this season to always come in its own way. Winter, too—my personal favorite. No matter what, the pumpkins will come out, the corn will be harvested, the apples picked, and then, out come the pine trees, snowmen, and mittens. I haven't personally experienced the festivities of either season, but it's a treat to watch it from a distance.

After the field and forests comes a small strip of stores. The entire strip is made of red brick and all the signs match, even the ones for chain places like Starbucks and McDonalds. Each sign is black with gold writing and makes everything look far posher than it truly is. We're driving fast, but I see glimpses of some local businesses—a pharmacy, a diner, some clothing stores—in addition to the chains. From what I can tell, everything seems pretty new, or maybe freshly refurbished. It comforts me it's less overwhelming than being in the city, with its densely populated streets and countless flashing signs. Seeing places I've never heard of is like a breath of fresh air, even though I'll probably never see any of these places again.

All kinds of different people bustle around with their shopping bags, families, and smiles. Every single person I see looks happy. This is familiar to them. It's home. They're just out getting a bite to eat or picking up a new jacket for the incoming winter. They'll be here for the new season and the one after that.

Thinking about the fact I probably won't be here for it makes my chest hurt, so I look away, focusing on my lap for the last couple of turns Jacob takes on the way to this new house. When we've arrived at the street, Jacob clears his throat.

"It should be on the right, I think. Look for number twelve," he tells me.

I pay little attention to the house numbers, though. I'm too busy staring at the white picket fences and manicured lawns. The street is deeply suburban, filled with sprawling lawns and presumably even further sprawling backyards. Though the sun is setting rapidly, I can tell the houses are well taken care of because of the way they seem to stand so proudly in their places, some adorned with early Christmas lights, some still with carved pumpkins.

When we're pulling into a driveway, I slowly lift my eyes. The first thing I notice is it is one of the houses with twinkly lights. They outline the roof and pillars on the porch, bright and creamy white. Just behind the house, the sky is filled with dark blue and a peachy color at the horizon, so the lights aren't so bright yet, but they still stand out. I look down the street to my right and notice several houses are outlined with the same warm light. I feel a pulse of pain run through my chest, though I cannot identify what it is.

The house has the routine mown lawn and several bare but towering trees surrounding it. The tallest of them is pine and filled with needles, shooting a few feet above the charcoal gray roof.

"Ready, Lavender?" Jacob says from my left, and my breath catches, but I nod and undo my seatbelt.

The late autumn air cuts through the rips in my flannel coat and makes me shiver as I get out of the car. I pull it tighter around me, walking to Jacob, who hands me my backpack and gives me a reassuring smile. I don't return it.

The pair of us walk single file up the gray stone path leading up to a towering door of deep brown wood, decorated with a wreath entwined with pinecones, golden leaves, and sunflowers. Jacob knocks above the wreath. My heart sinks to my stomach, then farther down, until it splatters out of the bottom of my feet, until I feel like I can't breathe. Jacob's face still has the idiotic smile. I stare straight ahead.

I try to ease my mind by reminding myself I've done this so many times, but all I can think is *Another failed placement. Another set of rules. Another bout of chores and responsibilities. Prepare yourself. Take a deep breath, and—*

The door swings open faster than the thought can fully form. "Oh, goodness, you guys are finally here! I was starting to worry you might've been caught in traffic on the highway. I thought I'd seen on the news there was an accident, and I'd hoped you wouldn't be stuck for hours!"

The woman before me has a brilliant, bold smile, framed with full lips and filled with straight, white teeth. Her face is deeply tanned, eyes so brown they're almost black, and her hair reaches her shoulders in soft waves. The crinkles by her warm eyes tell me her smile is genuine. My chest fills with ice at the prospect.

Not genuine. She's faking it for the social worker.

After Jacob fills the silence with short laughter, we are ushered into the house and I am coated in warmth. I'm looking at my shoes, so I first notice how filthy I am against the pristine hardwood floors, and I cringe without meaning to.

"So you must be Lavender!" my new foster mother exclaims at me, clasping her hands together. I can tell this is a true moment of joy for her.

"Obviously," I mumble.

Her smile falters, but Jacob has dealt with problem children too many times.

"Forgive us, Elise, it's been a long car ride and an even longer day. I'm afraid Lavender might be a little tired," he supplies.

"Oh, of course," Elise replies with a gentler smile than before. "Come in, both of you, and you can relax. Was the ride horrible? I know we're so far away from your office!"

I let the adults begin walking farther into the house. Crossing my arms across my chest, I follow them, but all I want is to be shown to my room so I can go to sleep and figure out how I'm going to survive this place.

Jacob continues the conversation with my new foster mother. I try my best not to feel like I'm going to throw up. As we get deeper into the house, I smell food being cooked;

something with a lot of garlic and, if I'm not mistaken, tomato sauce. I hear a television blaring, though not overly loud, and I am in awe of how far this family has gone to make it seem like I won't be treated like a criminal once the social worker leaves. The smiles, the cheeriness. It's a lot, to say the least. I roll my eyes but convince myself I'll be able to laugh about this when I'm alone later on.

Taking in the living room, the first thing I notice is a white and gray cat perched on the back of the couch, staring directly at me. I flinch but try to cover it up. The cat lets out a *meow* as if it's laughing at me and runs toward me. Before I know it, it's at my feet and rubbing against my dirty shoes.

"That's Hiro," a voice in front of me says. I look up to see two people staring at me intently.

A teenager and a child who looks to be around twelve are suddenly standing in front of me. The kid who spoke is a young girl.

She catches my eye and gives me the widest grin I've ever seen when I look up at her. I narrow my eyes inadvertently but only because I didn't know there would be someone so young here. Not only that, but she might be Elise's biological child, which I certainly did not anticipate. She has straight hair that drops a little past her shoulders, the same black as her mother's. It's messy on top. Her eyes are the same almost as black as her mother's, but I can't see much resemblance past that. She looks just like the boy, however. He's real tall, probably almost six-foot, with fluffy black hair that falls over his forehead in waves. His gray t-shirt advertises a band I've never heard of, and his jeans seem too small, but could also just be a style choice. Personally, I can't imagine wearing anything that clings to my skin that tightly.

"The cat," the girl says, throwing me out of my own mind. I realize I haven't responded to her. "His name is Hiro."

"Oh," is all I say. The cat seems to look up at me expectantly, but I tell him I don't have anything for him. This makes the girl and boy laugh, and I cross my arms defensively.

Elise notices the three of us have crossed paths and excitedly says, "Kai, Leia, I'd like you to meet someone very special. This is Lavender."

She gestures to me. This time, I huff out a laugh and roll my eyes so everyone can see. She's *got* to be kidding me.

"Just tell me where I sleep," I state lazily, not making eye contact with any of them. "Please," I add, but I'm sure it doesn't make me seem any less troubled.

Before anyone can answer, a middle-aged man comes forward from the kitchen to try and salvage the fading smiles and awkward silence. "Lavender, it's great to meet you. I'm Drew, Elise's husband. Leia would be happy to show you to your room as soon as we're finished with dinner, which should be done in about ten minutes. How does that sound?"

"Whatever."

The looks on Elise's and Drew's faces go from encouraging to uncertain, nervous. It confuses me since they both seem genuine. But I have nothing else to say, so I merely look at the floor and wait until the next time I'm spoken to.

"Elise, Drew, I apologize for Lavender's behavior. Like I said before, it's been a long day for her, and she's been through a lot these past couple of weeks. If you'll excuse us, I'll just have a word with her before I head out," Jacob explains kindly. I can tell he is merely trying to ease the situation and guaranteeing he won't get in trouble with CPS.

Jacob grabs my arm to walk me away from the family. The pressure of his hand around my arm just a little too tightly makes my heart clench uncomfortably, and before I know it, I'm shoving him off of me and demanding he lets me go. He stares at me in disbelief. His stare strays from my anger-filled face to my foster family, who coincidentally all decided the floor looks interesting right now.

"Lavender," Jacob says under his breath in a warning tone. I dare him with my fuming glare to reprimand me in front of these people, who he so wants to make a good impression on. I can tell his desire for the family to like him wins out as soon as he smiles at Elise and Drew, then walks in the opposite direction of them. I follow him.

We walk into a den to the right of the front door where it's nice and private. Jacob turns to me with anger in his eyes. "This is your last chance. You understand that, right?" he asks, pointing a finger at me.

I shrug.

Jacob takes a deep breath. With his eyes closed, he looks like he's meditating. I almost laugh. "Fine, Lavender. This is your life. Do you just want me to take you to the group home now?"

My eyes widen at the words. Something constricts in my chest that makes it hard to breathe. I can just barely say, "No."

Jacob's eyes have a knowing glint in them. "Exactly. Behave. I want this to be a positive experience for you."

"Fine."

He sighs and puts his pointer finger and thumb on the bridge of his nose. His face is bright red. Shaking his head, he says "okay" and tells me to head back to the family.

The family looks concerned but not discouraged. My face is blank as I walk to the living room, my arms crossed tightly across my chest. Jacob walks behind me. The family's cloudy expressions clear as we enter the room, and Elise walks toward us.

"Is everything okay?" she asks kindly.

Jacob quickly replies, "Of course. I'm sure Lavender will be feeling better by tomorrow."

I sigh loudly but I couldn't care less what Jacob or this family thinks. Sure, this is my "last chance" but I doubt I'll get myself kicked out with bad behavior. That's never what gets me. Whatever happens that gets me kicked out—and it will—won't be my fault. It's how it always is, but adults don't like to listen to me. Whatever.

Drew and Elise nod at me, as if I'm just so tired it's pitiable. Elise turns her attention back to Jacob.

"We aren't exactly sure how all of this works, so, will you be… staying for dinner?" she asks.

I start laughing because I think she's joking. When I realize she isn't, I start laughing harder.

Jacob ignores my outburst as I try to catch my breath. "No worries, Elise, but I'm afraid that would be inappropriate. My job is to just bring Lavender here and make sure she's good to go. I should be on my way now."

Elise's face is bright red, and she looks embarrassed. It dawns on me if she wasn't joking, she might be a first-time foster mother. Meaning she must be an idiot. Meaning they're *all* idiots for making this decision. Why let an unwanted child in when you have kids of your own? I guess they *could* be adopted, but it doesn't seem likely based on how much they all look alike.

Elise and Drew see Jacob out of the house and converse with him shortly before shutting the door behind him. Even though I have no emotional attachment to the guy, I feel the same pit in my stomach I always do when I'm officially alone in a new house.

Standing awkwardly in the hallway, I clear my throat to rid myself of the sad and lonely feeling that tries to settle on my shoulders, in my stomach, and in my throat.

This is normal. This always happens. It's no different now.

I'm ushered farther into the living room by Elise as Drew goes to check on dinner. It smells fine, I suppose. I take a guess it's probably spaghetti and meatballs and my theory proves to be correct when I see Drew straining the pasta over the sink. I look away as the steam seems to eat up his head and study the two children who have been standing stiffly in front of the couch.

Leia walks forward first and boldly stands in front of me, holding out her right hand. "Hi, Lavender. It's nice to meet you!"

With a furrow on my brow, I look at her, then down at her hand. Maybe it would be polite to shake it, but touching anyone, even this harmless girl, seems dreadful. So my arms stay crossed, and I look away from Leia without saying anything. In the corner of my eye, I notice she looks up at her brother, but it's of little interest to me.

In my peripheral vision, Kai nudges his sister. She stumbles on her words before getting out, "I'm really happy you're staying with us. I, uh, I've always wanted a sister. I mean, I like my brother, but I-I'm happy to have a sister now. Do you have any siblings?"

I look her in the eyes. She's trembling. Tilting my head to the side, I can't help but wonder why she would be. Still, I say, "Obviously not, or I wouldn't be here."

Her deep brown eyes grow round, and she shrinks back a little bit. It makes my heart ache. But my cold expression stays. The silence that settles between the three of us is deafening.

"Dinner is just about ready if you want to finish setting the table, Leia," Drew calls from the kitchen. I think he noticed the interaction. Leia walks to the kitchen without a word, and I'm left alone with the boy, Kai.

"So are you always this quiet?" he says immediately, almost as if he couldn't wait for his sister to leave.

I look up at him blankly. Even more silence is my response. I feel it's good enough to tell him exactly what he needs to know. Hopefully, he understands to leave me alone right from the beginning so I don't have to say something rude for him to back off.

"You're gonna have to talk at some point, you know," he continues. "My parents are gonna drive you crazy with questions during dinner. Whether you want to or not, they'll get an answer out of you."

We'll see about that.

I give him a scowl I reserve for people like him, who think they'll suddenly erase the years of experience I have in this sort of environment. I'm not going to magically become a different person just because this is a new house. I know what I know because of all those other houses that claimed they'd fix me.

The only difference is my icy exterior and scowl usually scare people away. After a while, they'll stop trying. I'm not saying Kai won't get tired of it eventually, but right now he just laughs at me, which is a new reaction entirely. It turns my stomach over and makes me feel uncomfortable.

"Come eat dinner," Kai says, smiling big. "It's Dad's specialty!" As confusion fills my face, Kai laughs again. "He's a terrible cook. Spaghetti really is the best it gets." He motions with his head for me to follow him.

With a sigh, I do, and I take the seat he gestures for me to take. I'm not hungry even though I haven't eaten yet today. The sight of a home-cooked meal usually excites me, even a little, because it's so uncommon for foster parents to cook for me. Spaghetti's my favorite food, too, but... all I want is to lay in a bed and rest. Even so, this will be a good opportunity to see how this family acts toward me once the social worker is out of the way.

Everyone goes about getting dinner ready in a way that tells me they have regular family dinners. Leia finishes setting the table with paper plates, silverware, and some glasses from a cupboard too high up for her to reach—Kai seems to anticipate this and brings them down before Leia can even ask.

Drew busies himself with bringing the food to the table on some wooden trivets that match the table. Simultaneously, Elise is getting drinks out of the refrigerator: a jug of water and a pitcher with what looks like iced tea.

"Lavender, do you drink soda?" Elise asks from across the kitchen.

I'm so lost in watching everyone move it takes me a second before I answer. "No."

She nods with a smile and proceeds to the table with just the water and tea. Almost all at once, the table is completely set and the family is sitting around me with forks in midair and glasses to their lips.

I chew slowly on the pasta that was served to me by Drew and try to avoid eye contact with everyone. For a few minutes, they seem to ignore me, which isn't unusual. I'd be let off easy if the worst these people did was ignore me.

Of course, I can't ever be that lucky.

"Lavender, I'm so excited to hear more about you," Elise begins. "You're our first foster and so I'm really curious to know about the types of places you've stayed at and how you ended up with us! Oh, I was just so thrilled when we got the call about you. I think it's real special you're our first, I mean, you're going to love it—"

I sigh loudly, throwing my fork down. "Will you just stop it? Stop acting like that!"

An uncomfortable silence settles over the five of us. Heat creeps up my neck and into my cheeks. I'm breathing heavily with a rage I can't explain. And even when I consult my brain, all it's telling me is I should feel this way and this is a necessary response to my environment.

"Honey, is something the matter?" Drew fills in.

I stare directly into his eyes. They look kind. But there's something more there, I just know it. He isn't kind. None of them are. They must be mocking me or something. Pretending to be nice so I get comfortable and let my guard down. *This* is something new.

"Yes, actually. Something is. I can't stand you people already."

I look at each and every one of them. Elise looks concerned, Drew like he's listening intently. Kai is smirking. Leia looks upset. I look away from her immediately.

"It's like freaking Disneyland in here. You people wouldn't know the *first* thing about me, and I intend on keeping it that way until you get sick of me and we both move on."

Elise clears her throat. Hesitantly, she asks, "Did something happen? Is there something we should know? I know Jacob mentioned you had a rocky past, but—"

"Shut up! Just *shut up*!" I'd prefer a hole in the head over talking about my *rocky past* to these people. Absolutely not. "I don't know what you thought this would be like, but *this* isn't it. You don't ask about what happened to me and I mind my business. You tell me what to do and I ignore it and you hate me and that's it. Just stop it."

This time, when the silence settles, I don't want to stick around for the conversation to be salvaged. I don't want to hear anymore from them. What kind of sick game are they playing with me?

"I'd like to go to my room. Please. Right now." I get up, avoiding eye contact.

"Lavender, we'd like it if you could finish dinner with us, so—"

Kai interrupts and says, "Mom, maybe we should let her rest. Her social worker said she's had a long day, so maybe this isn't the time to hound her with questions. All right?"

Elise hesitates, looking at her husband. They seem to communicate with their eyes. Finally, Elise nods, and Kai stands. He says he'll show me where my room is, and I get up to follow him. Grabbing my jacket and backpack, I keep my eyes lowered as I walk away.

Kai doesn't say a word to me as he leads the way up the wooden steps, to the left at the top, all the way to the end of the hallway, and to a bedroom away from everything else. "Bathroom's down the hall to the right. Your room's right there. If you need anything, just yell." He looks at me, eyes dripping with pity, and walks away.

Shaking my head at his back, I open the door to the room and find the light switch. Closing the door behind me, I do a once-over and swallow thickly. It's a big room, all white. White walls, white carpet. White bedspread.

With a sigh, I begin to change into sweatpants. My brain hurts too badly to think about this right now. Tomorrow. Tomorrow, I'll wake up and evaluate these people and what they're doing and, more importantly, what my role here is.

For now, I get under the white bedspread, which feels like clouds against my fingertips, and sink into the bed. After a deep, deep breath, I close my eyes.

CHAPTER TWO

When I wake up the next morning, it is in a cold sweat. I jolt out of the bed that's grown uncomfortably hot with my body heat and let myself catch my breath. I'm momentarily disoriented, unsure of where I am. Looking around, I expect to see the dark green, peeling wallpaper of my last foster home, but of course, all I see is the pristine white painted walls of this new room. It doesn't overwhelm my senses like the green did. Instead, I'm able to hear myself think loud and clear.

I peel the comforter from my legs and stand up, rubbing my temples to erase the images that cannot be erased. I squint against the sun that pours through two windows against the back wall of the room. They are covered merely by sheer white blinds and do little to hide the strong, early-morning glow. My eyes hurt from the presence of the daylight, and I am visited once again by that pesky headache that settles into the middle of my forehead. I take deep breaths slowly until I'm breathing fine, but pain refuses to go away.

With one final, deep sigh, I decide it'd be best if I cleaned myself up. It's only eight o'clock in the morning on this sunny Saturday, and I can't imagine anyone else is awake, which should save me from any awkward encounters on the way to the bathroom.

As soon as I open the door, I realize I have misjudged the Kahales entirely.

The sound of clattering dishes and hushed, groggy tones floats up to me along with the sweetness of what I assume to be pancakes or waffles. My stomach gives a violent grumble in response. Rubbing my eyes hard, I silently curse this family solely for the fact they have the nerve to be up at the same time as me. Even so, I make my way to the bathroom and freshen up the best I can without using a shower since I haven't been told how to yet.

I comb my fingers through my hair, use some strong mouthwash that was on the counter, and splash my face with cold water. My skin looks dull and gray, my eyes nearly black and blue. But this is the best I can do right now, so I leave the bathroom grumpily.

If I weren't so starved, I'd probably go right back to my room, but my traitorous stomach drags me downstairs, where I fall into a pit of morning positivity I can't stand.

Immediately, I'm pestered with a good morning from everybody, even Kai, who looks like he's about to fall asleep on the tub of butter sitting in front of him. Everyone's got messy hair and sleepy eyes, but they all look happy to be eating breakfast together.

Hiro the cat, however, seems to have the same thought as me while he snoozes on the couch, paws splayed out underneath him. I can hear him snoring from the kitchen.

With my eyebrows scrunched together, I mutter, "Morning," to the Kahales, standing awkwardly.

Am I just supposed to invite myself to their table? I suppose I should be used to moments like this, but I can't say I've ever been in a situation where I wasn't being told what to do. It's always "*You'll sit here*, or *Take your food to your room*." I haven't been able to choose a seat myself before.

But the Kahales are staring and I'm staring back for too long, so I quickly take the same seat I used at dinner, feeling stupid for not knowing the way around these people yet.

Without saying anything, Drew hands me a dish and starts piling it high with pancakes. I dig in without another thought, forgetting to even thank him. I can only focus on how hungry I am.

I'm halfway through my third pancake when I realize everyone's *still* staring at me. "What? Do I have to ask first or something?"

Leia laughs. It's the first time I've seen her without a serious expression on her face. Her teeth are slightly crooked, and her smile ages her down a few years somehow. Her resting face makes her seem much more mature.

I'm intrigued by the change in her attitude. This morning, she at least seems less nervous than last night, though I don't know what *she* had to be nervous about.

"Ask?" she asks with a giggle. "To eat breakfast?"

My face heats with embarrassment, and any interest in her falls away like dried leaves shaken off a branch. I'd let my guard slip with that meager ounce of curiosity, and look where it's already gotten me: humiliated. No wonder she doesn't understand why I'd have to ask if I can eat. No one ever would. I get it, she's young, but how could she be so naïve? How could you live a life *so good* you can't even imagine other people living lives anything less than perfect? Hadn't her parents prefaced my arrival with *anything?*

"Well, I've had to ask before, so you can wipe that smile off your face," I snap, staring her in the eyes.

She stops smiling, but her eyes widen. She looks uncertainly at her parents, one at a time. Then her eyes find mine again. "You... you have? But why?"

I roll my eyes and cut into my pancakes once again. This isn't a conversation I want to have, so I won't.

After a few seconds of my silverware clattering, everyone else's clattering joins mine and the topic is dropped. I hope selfishly all conversations are dropped, but unfortunately, I'm not *that* lucky.

"Lavender, how did you sleep last night?" Elise asks over her coffee mug. "Did you find everything okay? Pillows, blankets? I didn't know how many of each you'd want, so I just put a bunch in the room. There's even more in the closet if you didn't already check it."

"Yeah," I reply vaguely. I don't have the brain capacity to even comprehend all the things she just said.

"Damn. She has a worse attitude than *me*, and that's saying something," Kai says from my left. He laughs, and I look at him with pure anger dripping from my glare.

It only makes him laugh harder.

"Kai, that isn't nice," Elise says. "Lavender is just adjusting to a new home. Of course, it makes sense she'd be a bit grumpy. When we took you home from the hospital, you cried for months. I'd prefer anything to that constant wailing."

Kai lets out an exasperated chuckle. "I was a newborn baby! That's what newborn babies do!"

"I didn't cry all the time," Leia chimes in, holding her fork up. "Mom says I was a good baby."

"That doesn't mean you didn't cry, and *you did*. I remember." Kai seems to realize something and scoffs. "You still *are* a baby, Leia!"

"Am not!"

The two of them start bickering incessantly over me. I stare at them with blatant confusion, and when I notice Drew and Elise laughing quietly to themselves, my confusion burns deeper.

What kind of family is this?

It's weird enough they decide to foster children when they have some of their own, but it's like they're... like they're just *not normal.* I mean, this is weird, right? No normal family acts like this, talking over each other, making jokes all day. No normal family sits down for breakfast together early in the morning on a Saturday. At least, no normal family does so *happily.*

Finally, Elise chimes in and tells Kai and Leia to quiet down and finish their breakfast.

"I'm not hungry anymore," Leia blurts out, looking nervous and fidgety. She sets her fork down with a clatter.

"Really? You barely ate anything, sweetheart. Are you sure you're finished?" Elise asks, worried.

Leia nods and shrugs. "I'm just not hungry today."

"You're not going to get hungry on the way to soccer practice, are you? We won't have time to stop for something," her mother continues in a warning tone.

"I promise, I'm fine."

Elise nods and tells Leia to head up to her room to get changed for soccer practice, which begins at 9:30 a.m. It could very well be why they're all awake, but I'd rather not ask. In fact, I'd love to avoid all contact with this family as a whole as much as possible.

I sigh and dig back into my pancakes. I'm still hungry and debate on whether I should dig into Leia's leftovers, too, but I decide I'd probably get in trouble for something like that and stick to my own plate.

As I keep eating, Elise takes a deep sip of her coffee, Drew begins clearing plates, and Kai scrolls through his phone.

"Lavender, would you like anything else?" Drew asks from the sink.

Even though I could probably eat a thousand more pancakes, I shake my head.

"Kai, did you tell Lavender about tomorrow night?" Elise asks, and my shoulders tense. I can't imagine what I could already be involved in.

"No, I didn't." He locks his phone with an exhale and turns to me, his face serious. "I'm going out with some friends tomorrow night and, um..." He looks at his mom, who nods encouragingly. "Mom thought it would be a good opportunity for you to get familiar with the town, so you can come along with me, meet all my friends, see where we normally hang out."

I swallow hard and keep my eyes on the kitchen table. Though my heart races, my voice is steady when I ask, "Why would I do that?"

"It would make the transition into school a little smoother, I think," Elise says. "You might not know Kai's friends so well, but at least they'll be familiar faces when you get to school on Monday. What do you say?"

She barely finishes her sentence before I mutter, "No."

Elise just sighs lightly and leans forward so she's practically forcing me to look up. I do, but I can't look her in the eye. "I know this is all scary, honey, I do. I know this is the millionth new school for you, but this will be good for you. I promise."

She *promises*? What good is that for me? I barely know this woman, and she's already making promises she can't keep, she doesn't know *how* to keep. And for what? So I'll trust her and unwittingly fall into her and her family's trap?

But what *is* the trap? What are they trying to do? Maybe they want me unguarded so they can fix me, just like all the other foster parents have tried to. But they always try to fix me by enforcing strict rules and screaming at me. That doesn't seem to be the case here—yet, at least—so this is a tactic I'm unfamiliar with.

In the end, however, they want to fix me, which is what everyone else wants to do. It is exactly the kind of thing I refuse to subject myself to. I will not be fixed by these people. I won't be whipped into a well-mannered idiot who allows herself to be taken advantage of. Because that's what they want. If I'm well-mannered, they can do whatever they want to me. They can keep me here. Keep me in this system that has taken *everything* from me—my happiness, my sanity, my dignity. My parents, whoever and wherever they may be.

It doesn't matter if these people will try to do this with a smile or snarl on their face—in essence, this is the same thing, but it is unfamiliar, which makes it toxic for me.

So I have to get out.

As I shovel the last bite of pancakes into my mouth, I try my hardest to stare Elise in the eye. I'll comply with what she wants, only so I can understand the full situation. I have to know how to get out of this school, this town, not just this home. Maybe if I force myself to endure a terrifying social interaction, I'll know all I need to know.

"Fine," I say stonily. My heart has not stopped racing from before. Now, my palms begin to sweat, and I put down my fork. "I'll go."

Elise is delighted, of course, and Kai gives me a small smile. I can tell he isn't thrilled about this himself. But he's still making me do it. Without saying anything else, I clench my jaw and walk away.

CHAPTER THREE

Kai could very well be the bane of my existence. He obviously only invited me to this little gathering because his mom forced him, but that isn't stopping him from bothering me every moment of this car ride. It's like he's on special assignment from Elise to drive me insane, and it's certainly working.

"Come on, just sing one line! *Please!*" Kai begs me, and I sigh for the millionth time. My arms are crossed so tightly against my chest they've begun to go numb.

"I know you listen to this in your free time, Lavender, I know it!"

"Shut up, Kai!" I snap, but this only eggs him on. He laughs like it's a game, like him getting on my nerves is only furthering his need to keep going.

Kai taps on the steering wheel to the Taylor Swift song blaring throughout his car. I would die in a hole before admitting I used to sing the song into my hairbrush when I was nine, not because the music isn't good, but because he's embarrassing me. Being nine years old, I never got many moments to be on my own. And being tossed from foster home to foster home, I didn't get to truly be myself at all.

But one night, my foster family at the time left me at home. By myself. Maybe it's cruel to leave a kid that young alone, but it had felt like I won the lottery at the time. They'd only gone to dinner—it was a relative's birthday, and since I wasn't their family, I didn't belong at something like that—but those two hours were defining moments for me. I logged into their desktop computer and found my way onto YouTube—the social workers at CPS sometimes let me mess around on their computers when I was waiting there for a long time. The only song I knew at the time was "Love Story," so I searched it, grabbed my cracked purple hairbrush, and sang my little heart out.

As I'm deep in this memory, I almost smile, but I'm drawn back to reality at the sound of Kai's pitchy declaration of love for Romeo.

I stare out my window into the darkening sky, trying to shake off the past. It isn't late, but because of the incoming winter, the sky grows dark earlier now. I like it better this way. It reminds me of the promise of snow.

"Why are you in such a bad mood?" Kai asks, not unkindly. He sounds genuine enough and clearly doesn't mean to pry, but I can't help but wonder why he'd even care.

"Maybe because I'm being dragged to a *thing* I don't want to go to."

"Well, why didn't you stay home, then?"

I turn my head to look at him confusedly. "You and your mother acted like it wasn't an option. If it was, I'd like you to turn around. Right now."

Kai giggles. "You're fun to tease. Has anyone ever told you that?"

I scoff, rolling my eyes. "I wish you'd shut up."

"And I wish you'd admit you like me and think I'm gonna be the coolest brother ever," he playfully remarks, and my stomach clenches.

As I look at him again, I secretly hope he thinks I look intimidating, because I don't feel intimidating at all. No one's ever called themselves my sibling before, and it's really weird and throws me off. He has no business acting like I'd ever be close to him, he'd ever be that close to me. Doesn't he understand my role here? Doesn't he get I'm not his family? I'll always be an outsider?

"Are you stupid?" I snap. "Or are you just trying to make me angrier than I already am?"

"Whoa!" He holds up a hand in defense and keeps his eyes on the road. I focus on the clicking of the car's turning signal so I don't get *too* angry. "Why am I *stupid*? I'm just trying to get to know you and you're giving me nothing here."

"Yes, you're right. I'm giving you nothing because I don't *want* you to know me. I don't like you, and I certainly don't care if you like me. And you are *not* my brother, nor will you ever be."

For once, silence fills the car. Even the radio is quieter, probably because Kai turned it down when I wasn't paying attention. I take a deep breath and try my best to ignore the pounding of my heart. I blink hard, tense my muscles for a second, and furrow my brow. I repeat these things until I don't feel overwhelmed with the nervousness that's settled in my stomach and chest.

"I'm sorry, then," he mumbles. He seems to deflate, a wilted flower, and I swallow hard at the implication I hurt his feelings. I know I did, and I know it was uncalled for.

He's silent for the rest of the ride. He doesn't even tap along to the next song that comes on. I know I've hurt him, but I can't care about that. Becoming emotionally invested in any way in Kai will make it harder to do what I need to do to get out of here. Why has he been trying so hard, anyway? What's the big deal?

I try to stop thinking about it as Kai pulls into a parking spot on the side of the street. We're in the middle of town, but cars are parked all along the streets.

Both of us get out of the car without a word. I follow Kai to the left and look at the stores to my right as we walk by them. They all look brand new, for some reason, with their extra bright lights and all-white interiors. My eye catches on a vintage clothing store because it is noticeably darker than all the rest of the stores. I also notice a few tiny antique stores amongst all of the other chain stores you'd find anywhere.

After walking past several stores, we reach the corner of the block, and 1960s music floods my ears. The diner emits a neon blue and purple glow that separates itself entirely from the rest of the street. Along with the music, the hearty sound of endless overlapping chatter fills the air as we get closer. People stand outside, some smoking cigarettes, some parting ways with the rest of their group, some waiting to be seated. It seems like a very popular place to be tonight and also seems like a place I really, *really* don't want to be. I haven't been in many restaurants since my previous foster parents have never wanted to pay for me to eat out. I'm not used to being around so many people, and as soon as we walk inside, I know this was a huge mistake.

The first thing I hear is a child crying. Next is the clatter of silverware and dishes, someone laughing loudly, and people slurping their drinks. Looking around with wide eyes, I see the neon lights adorn the entirety of the place. Pink lights surround the whole ceiling and turn everyone's faces a bit purple.

"Are you all right?" Kai asks me. He's staring at me with uncertainty.

"I'm fine." I look down at my shoes. Being overwhelmed by a diner probably makes me an idiot.

I follow Kai through the main section of the diner and weave carefully through the field of metal chairs and checkerboard tables. We eventually arrive at a huge booth, at which two girls and a boy already sit.

Kai's face completely changes as he sees his friends. His smile reaches his eyes as he greets them with a loud hello. They each greet him with the same energy and seem delighted he has finally arrived. Once their eyes find me, their excitement falters, and I look away.

"Oh, hey, guys," Kai begins. Is his excitement now feigned, or am I imagining things? "Remember how I told you my parents decided to become foster parents? We got our first foster kid. This is Lavender."

"Dope name," one of the girls remarks with a smile. Her white, straight teeth contrast beautifully with her lips, which are covered in a dark berry gloss. Her skin is tawny and warm, lit with the neon lights, making her appear as if she's glowing. "I'm Jane."

I nod as my heart races, giving her the weakest smile of my life. I look like the equivalent of a trash bag in her presence.

"I'm Michael," the boy to Jane's right greets me with a wave. His whole body seems to move with the rapid bouncing of his leg. He has dyed red hair the color of a firetruck and kind eyes.

"Marisa," the last girl says, a bit more reserved, but her smile is just as warm and welcoming. Her hair is long and dark brown, skin clear and nearly perfect.

What kind of people are these? They look like they all just walked off of a set, or maybe I'm just used to looking terrible.

"Nice to meet you guys," I mumble.

There is a beat of silence as they realize I'm not as enthusiastic as them about this introduction. Then, the girl named Jane interrupts the silence.

"So you're in foster care, right?" she asks with a hint of misplaced excitement. "You must have some really unique perspectives of this country."

I look at her and try to ignore the kindness and genuine curiosity in her voice. "Is that what they're calling abuse these days? A *unique perspective*? Interesting, I haven't heard that one yet."

Kai seems to choke on air. Michael looks surprised. The two girls give each other a look I cannot identify, but it makes my stomach turn.

"You're kinda right, Lavender," Michael says hesitantly. "Jane, you have no idea what shit she's seen."

Jane shakes her head, face unguarded and apologetic. "You're completely right. That was insensitive. I suppose I'm just curious to know about the system. You know, we don't learn about it much, and it isn't every day you meet someone who's been through what you have."

I shake my head in response. "Kids like me are everywhere. You just aren't looking hard enough."

Before anyone can say anything else, a waiter comes to the table. He's blond and blue-eyed, taller than Kai, and has a black lip ring.

"Hey, guys. Can I get you anything to drink?" the waiter asks. He doesn't have a notepad; instead, he holds his hands behind his back as he leans to hear our orders.

"Hey, Luke," Kai says. He reaches over me and taps his knuckles to the waiter's. I watch as Michael, Jane, and Marisa collectively roll their eyes and make note of it. "I'll have a Coke, please."

Everyone else orders their drinks, and Luke's eyes land on me. As he notices me for the first time, his face turns quizzical.

"You're new," Luke says matter-of-factly, as if I'm a new pair of shoes he's admiring. "Who are you?"

"She's my foster sister, Luke," Kai interjects.

"Foster sister, huh? That's interesting." Luke rests his palms on the table and leans forward even further. "Can I get your name?"

I let the fakest smile I can muster fill my face. "No."

Luke laughs hesitantly. "No?"

Marisa says, "She said no, asshat. Go get my water."

But Luke doesn't tear his eyes away from me. "I'll give you free fries if you tell me your name."

"You're bribing me? To know my name?" I roll my eyes as he nods stupidly. "I hate fries. And men."

His eyebrows shoot up so far his forehead is practically swallowed up. "No way. You're a—"

"Please go away," Kai finally interjects. When I look at him, his neck is red and his face is buried in his hands. Even though I'm equally as embarrassed, it's nice to see Kai squirming instead of being perfect.

"Yes, *please*, because—" I try to say, but I'm interrupted by a new voice.

"Oh, Kai, what did I tell you about bothering Luke over here? You know he's fragile!"

Luke spins around to defend his masculinity but falters when he sees who it is. "Emerson, did you know she's a lesbian?"

"I never said I was *anything*," I fume, my hands balling into fists in my lap. I can feel the heat in my cheeks, the adrenaline rushing through me that comes with the unfamiliar feeling of speaking up for myself. "Me hating men has absolutely nothing to do with my sexuality. Not to mention how much it is *not* your business."

The girl behind Luke—Emerson—moves closer to our table, so I can see her better. When I do, my heart jumps to my throat and I swallow thickly, wishing for water right now. My adrenaline rush seems to speed further, the blood rumbling in my ears. For a moment, all I see is this girl in front of me, and I have to blink several times to eradicate the tunnel vision. I clench my jaw, taking in her expression, which is hard in several ways but soft in several more. She's quite simply very beautiful, her brow furrowed defiantly, lips lifted in a lovely smirk.

Emerson gently shoves Luke out of the way so she's in front of me, leaning against the table and staring right into my eyes. I feel a fluttering in my stomach, but I furrow my brow just like hers, hoping it remotely resembles that glare.

Her face is filled with soft angles. She has one of those cute noses that rounds at the bottom, with the perfect slope in between her two round, dark eyes. Her auburn hair is pulled into a tight, high ponytail that shows off a soft jawline and slender shoulders. I swallow again.

Before she can get a word out—who knows if I'd be able to stay conscious if she did—I blurt out, "I think your boyfriend needs to mind his manners."

Emerson's lips break into a smile as she doubles over with genuine laughter. "You're way off, love. As you like to put it... I *hate men*. I wouldn't be interested in Luke."

I do not let my stony expression fall with the descent of my stomach to the floor. Perhaps I've laid it on too thickly this time, but I'm not used to this much attention. It's all Kai's fault for making me come here. I can't help but be defensive to people who invade my space and insist on talking to me like Emerson, Luke, and even Kai's friends. I've never done something like this, and I know I'm doing it all wrong, but once my attitude is running my brain, it's all that can come out. Unfortunately, these people are too civil to say anything rude back to me. That would make this so much easier.

"Whatever," I respond lamely. It's the only word that appears in my head. I'm completely off my game because of all the eyes on me, and Emerson knows it.

She snickers and begins to walk away. With one last look at me, Luke walks away as well, but I know I'll be seeing him again tonight.

As silence once again settles at the table, I let myself tune into the music playing throughout the place. I think it's The Beatles. I focus on it so I don't have to think about what just happened, what I *let* happen. I already know too many people here. Soon, Kai Kahale and his entire family will start thinking I'm getting integrated, and soon after, they'll think they've fixed me because I'll be social and lovely and go to idiotic high school parties and football games. The thought alone makes me sick to my stomach.

"So are we gonna talk about how insanely weird that was, or no?" Jane finally says. I look at her and laugh humorlessly, lightly, and everyone else joins in.

"I'd prefer we forget about it," I say honestly.

"Probably a good idea," Michael reinforces. "Have you told her about Emerson yet, Kai?"

Kai shakes his head, laughing uncomfortably. He reached back and scratches his neck, which has grown red and hot. "Not something I ever really want to talk about, but..." He seems to falter, but continues, "Well... I crushed on her from first grade until freshman year. It was pathetic, really. And when I say pathetic, I mean it. I'd get her a Valentine every

Valentine's Day and she would just say, 'Thanks.' Every time. On Valentine's Day in freshman year, when I handed her a rose, she screamed, 'I'm gay! I like girls!' in the middle of the hallway. And that was the only time she ever came out, and she never talked about it again and everyone just knew. So I essentially turned her gay, and that will be my legacy until I die."

Everyone laughs except for me. Sure, it's a cute story or whatever, but Kai is giving himself too much credit. He didn't do anything to Emerson. Emerson had always been gay, but Kai couldn't take no for an answer in first grade through freshman year, so she was forced to admit it at that point.

"You're such a try-hard," I blurt out, without really meaning to.

"Huh?"

"You tried to get a girl to like you for eight years. The same girl. And when she ended up trying to get rid of you, you turned on her like she did something awful. Am I wrong?"

Kai clears his throat and looks down at his lap as the rest of the table contains their laughter. I've struck a nerve. Again. Whoops. I can't say I care much. I think he deserved to hear that. It's selfish of me, but I won't have to deal with this drama once I'm out of here in a matter of days, thank God. In the meantime, I may as well stir the pot a bit. I'm already doing such a great job, it's my third day here, and I'm involved in drama. As I sit at this diner booth, my plan unfolds before me.

CHAPTER FOUR

The sound of a rumbling *meow* wakes me up. Opening my eyes abruptly, I am surprised by the image of Hiro's shining yellow orbs. The white and gray cat appears to have settled in on my chest, and he glares at me with visible judgment, as if my sheer terror bothers him immensely. I shove him off unceremoniously and he gives me an ungrateful yelp. Feeling the lingering nightmare dissipate from my mind, the sheer terror in my brain flooding every one of my senses, I scrub at my face indignantly. I already cannot remember my dream, but my body does. The pounding of my heart forces me upright as I inhale and exhale shakily.

The only flash of memory I have from the nightmare is the color blue and the scratch of concrete against my hands and knees. Even these minuscule details from a place I hardly recognize fill me with a sense of dread. I drop my head into my hands and steady my breathing.

What a wonderful way to wake up on a school day.

Not only a school day, but my first day at Springfield South. Not only that, but today will commence the beginning of my plan to get out of this house—likely my last if my social worker was serious about sending me to a group home.

Though the plan took very little effort to construct, it will take effort to complete. The Kahales are very obviously tolerating my bad behavior, but to get kicked out, I have to push it a little further than I already have. I have to find the limit and go past it. The result will undoubtedly be the group home I've been promised, which, despite being the worst place to end up, has to be better than here. If not better, then the same as my previous foster homes, which are a step up from this place.

I rub my sleepy eyes and stand up. Hiro makes himself comfortable in the warm spot on the bed, and I scoff. I slept through the night, but I feel even more tired than before I went to bed. Dragging my exhausted body toward the bedroom door, I silently beg for a quick day so I can go back to sleep.

Once in the bathroom, it takes me a few seconds to adjust to the bright light, so I decide to sit on the floor until I feel like getting up. As it turns out, this only makes me almost fall asleep again, so several minutes pass before I hear a banging on the bathroom door followed by Kai's voice telling me to hurry up. I know I'm running scarily late by now, but I take my time while brushing my teeth and washing my face. Maybe the Kahales won't like it if I'm tardy, and maybe they'll get so annoyed they'll stop talking to me at some point.

After washing my face, I give myself a good, hard look in the mirror. My face is deathly pale, almost gray, and my brown eyes are wan, nearly black in the fluorescent light. Maybe when I was younger I was pretty, with my blond hair and fair skin, but now I just look like a zombie. It upsets me, but I remember what I look like is of no concern to me right now. I have to focus on getting out of here.

I might not be as unfocused as I thought, considering Elise starts yelling up to me only a few minutes after I'm back in my room. I'm practically ready for school, but Elise has only given me a five-minute warning, so I move even slower.

I know I've pushed it when Elise is knocking on my bedroom door and telling me Leia will miss her bus, which will make Kai and me even later to school, or which will make Elise late to work. Kai tends to drive Leia to her bus stop, see, but if she misses the bus, it's up to Elise and Kai to take her to school. Elise does not seem happy about either option from the way her nostrils flare and her cheeks heat up, but she doesn't raise her voice at me. She merely tells me to be a little quicker tomorrow morning, to wake up a little earlier, so we don't have this problem again.

I respond with, "Whatever," which I know bothers her. Adults hate that word.

I feel bad when I see how panicked Leia looks when I finally get downstairs, though. Elise decides to take her herself, and as Leia gets into her mom's car, she looks on the verge of tears. I think I might hear Elise trying to calm her down, but I can't be sure. That was *my* doing—upsetting an innocent girl—and it hurts me to know I'm acting like this, but it's okay, right? I'm doing this to prevent myself from being in a toxic living environment. People have done worse for worse.

When I'm in Kai's car, he asks me why I was running late. Instead of telling him I had a nightmare and needed to calm down, I say, "What's the big deal? I just wanted to sleep in."

He laughs humorlessly and gives me a look. "Seriously?"

I don't answer him because, again, I feel like a bad person and I no longer want to talk about it.

The ride to school is simple and short, so the dread inside of me grows quickly, spreading throughout every crevice of my body. This is a familiar feeling, so I don't entirely shut down. In fact, this morning has been filled with less stress than usual. I'm not used to being driven to school; usually I'm meant to take a bus, but since Kai is a senior, he gets to have his car and apparently doesn't mind driving me. I'm willing to bet his mother forced him to just like she forced him to take me out and meet his friends, but that's beside the point.

After parking, Kai says, "I'll walk you to the office so you can get your schedule and paperwork, okay?"

"Fine," I say dryly.

Walking into this new school, I don't see many differences from the other schools I've been to. Of course, city schools look a lot different, but every high school has the same essence for some reason. However, Springfield High School is most definitely the richest school I've been to. The exterior looks almost like a modern office building, and inside it doesn't smell like dirty socks and wooden pencils, but it does smell like the first day of school, whatever that smell really is.

Kai and I walk through hallways lined with tall, navy blue lockers. Students hang around in the hallways, sitting on the floor, catching up on homework, talking to their friends. I notice Kai smiling or waving at a few students who greet him in return and wonder distantly if he's popular.

As we get further into the building, it gets a bit noisier. At the heart of the school are the cafeteria and a small room that serves coffee to teachers and students, which is unlike anything I've ever seen before. To me, it's more reminiscent of a college building, which kind of weirds me out. Why does everything have to be so different here?

Students milling about near the cafeteria are louder and way more enthusiastic than necessary. I hear someone playing music, which is a detail that never fails to be present at any public high school I've been to, and the individual cliques are very obvious here. I note it, but present myself as disinterested.

Kai opens the door of the office for me and gestures for me to go inside. I do and turn around to see if he's leaving, but he follows me inside.

"You don't have to stay with me," I say.

"Don't you want me to show you to your classes?" he asks with a furrow of his dark brows, his hands spread.

"What? No. Don't you have to go to your *own* classes?"

He looks confused and hesitant to leave. I cross my arms over my chest, hardening my face so he knows I'm serious.

"Leave, Kai," I finally blurt. But it seems harsh, so I add, "I'm fine."

"Are you sure?"

Sighing dramatically, I snap, "Just go! What's the big deal?"

I knew he'd be a pain but I didn't think *these* sorts of things would be an issue. I get it, he wants to get out of class or whatever, but really? Why won't he just leave me alone? Orders from his mother, I presume.

"Whatever," he mutters pointedly and turns and leaves.

Which obviously leaves me in a new place by myself. I hadn't considered this before I forced him away. I've been in situations like this countless times and the anxiety of it will never cease. But I would never allow Kai—or anyone, for that matter—to stay around me like that for no reason. I'll find my way, or I won't, and either way, it will be fine because this school doesn't matter. Neither does Kai.

I approach the woman at the front desk and introduce myself halfheartedly. She points me in the direction of the principal's office after handing me a folder of papers, including my schedule and the school handbook. I make my way to the principal's office and, once inside, listen to her give me an overly fervent pep talk that doesn't resonate with me at all. In fact, as soon as I leave her office, I can't remember a word she said.

The only thing I *do* remember is I have to make a right after leaving the office to get to my first class, which is PE. After the right, though, there's just a blank space in my brain.

I try walking down one hallway because it seems like it would lead to the gym, but it doesn't. I turn around and start over, pick a new hallway, but once again, I end up at more classrooms. After this, I simply don't feel like looking for the gym, partly because gym classes tend to be really annoying but also partly just because I don't want this school day to start.

Instead, I'll wander for now, maybe find my other classes, and plan a walking route. Why do I need PE anyway?

The first bell rings as I'm rounding a corner, and a flood of students rushes toward me. I decide to follow the crowd for a bit before picking my own route and hugging the hallway so as not to stand out. There's a lot of kids at this school, and I haven't caught anyone's eye just yet.

I keep walking until I arrive at a stairwell, which seems like a perfect place to sit down. It's out of the way and completely empty right now since everyone is pretty much in their respective classes. I sit for a bit and shut my eyes, try to rationalize my behavior, and I think I'm partially successful. I don't *want* to go to class, and since I need to get kicked out of this town, why should I go to class? I can think of more reasons why I shouldn't, which makes me feel a little better about the whole thing. At the same time, I cannot wholly ignore the guilt writhing in my stomach, begging me to think this through.

I swallow hard as my throat seems to tighten, looking up at the ceiling. What kind of person have I turned into? I can't remember when the switch happened, when I went from trying my very best to be a good little girl, to excelling in school and trying to make foster parents proud so they would take me in permanently, to the person I am today. Have I even given the Kahales a real chance? Have I given any foster homes a real chance these past couple of years?

But there is a nagging in me that tells me where I am right now is not where I'm meant to be. The Kahales aren't my "forever home" and there is a very real feeling in my gut this really is just another tactic they're using to change me and hurt me in some way. I refuse to be hurt by another foster family.

Perhaps this different approach they have is the reason why I feel so unsettled. In the past, I have been hurt so upfront from the beginning because of the way the homes have been run—harsh punishments, locks on cabinets and refrigerators, missing bedroom doors. The Kahales aren't like that, so there must be something up their sleeves I just haven't been exposed to yet.

When I can't stand the racing of my mind, the restlessness coursing through me, I stand and begin walking around again. At least when I'm moving, I can focus on classroom numbers and people watching and counting floor tiles. Anything other than the negative thought spiral that threatens to eat me alive.

I turn down a new hallway and notice two students walking toward me. As I get closer, I realize with horror I recognize them.

It's the auburn hair that gives it away.

Emerson and Luke walk side by side, talking quietly to each other. They're both smirking. They don't yet see me, and I highly consider turning around and walking in the opposite direction so they never see me. But I unfortunately don't get the chance, because Luke suddenly looks up and spots me.

His eyes widen, and he immediately points at me like I'm an animal at the zoo. Emerson follows his finger and her eyes land on me. They squint as she laughs out loud and walks toward me, and that tight feeling in my throat returns. The mere sight of her makes me feel like I'm choking on air, and I wish briefly the ground could swallow me whole.

"Fancy meeting you here," she says matter-of-factly. She holds an iced coffee dripping with condensation.

My only response is a tight, fake smile. I can tell Emerson gets joy from my response, for whatever reason.

"Shouldn't you be in class?" she asks me.

I scoff. "Shouldn't *you*?"

"Obviously. But I needed to use the bathroom."

I look around dramatically. "This doesn't look like the bathroom, Emerson."

Her smile drops to a playful smirk as she takes one step forward. Luke looks on with a stupid grin on his face. "You know what's weird? I still don't know your name."

Shrugging, I respond, "Is that weird? I don't think it is, since I don't intend on telling you my name. If you want to know so badly, I'm sure you'll figure it out."

The smile returns to Emerson's face, and I'm surprised to see it seems genuine, like she thinks we're playing a little game here she's thoroughly enjoying. Maybe I'm playing into it without even realizing it, and I can't say I mind. Maybe it's even fun for me. And so what if it is? I'll be out of here soon enough.

"You're funny. And I *will* find out your name."

My eyes move to Luke slowly. "Why don't you have your *boyfriend* find out for you?"

Emerson shakes her head with that little smile on her face still. "You must not have heard me last night, but Luke is *not* my type. I'd be willing to spell it out for you if you think it's necessary, but I—"

"Hey, Lavender, is everything okay over here?"

I spin around promptly, my cheeks aflame and my eyes wide. Michael, Kai's friend, comes strolling up to the three of us, looking concerned.

Emerson is laughing too hard for my liking. I know it's because she heard my name, though I was hoping it was only me who heard Michael screaming down the hallway at me.

"I barely had to work for it, Lavender." The way she says my name makes my stomach hurt. I feel my shoulders tense uncomfortably.

When Michael's standing next to me, I turn to him and say, "Everything's fine, Michael, but thank you for your concern."

He doesn't look convinced. "Are they bothering you or something?"

I furrow my brow. "No, they aren't *bothering* me. Why aren't *you* in class?"

He shrugs innocently. "Bathroom."

I sigh and look away. Emerson is smirking playfully at me, and Luke is still smiling like an idiot. I wonder if he knows at all what's going on, but the vacant look in his eyes tells me he is entirely away from here.

"What are you four doing in the hallway?"

All of our heads turn to see a teacher looking at us with a suspicious and angry glare on her face. She's old and wearing the ugliest maroon skirt I've ever seen in my life.

When none of us answers, she asks impatiently, "Can I see your hall passes, please?"

Of course, Michael, Emerson, and Luke all lift up their purple hall passes, and I simply look the teacher in her old, wrinkled face with an expression I hope seems unassuming and harmless.

"Why don't you have a pass?"

Her eyes bore holes into my skull, but the lie comes easily to my lips. "It's my first day here and I got lost trying to get to my first class. My foster brother said he would help me find it, but he abandoned me as soon as the bell rang. These three generous students saw me wandering and offered to help me find my way."

Michael, Emerson, and Luke all stare at me and try not to laugh, but I don't let it show on my face I'm lying. It would ruin what I have going, and I can't let that happen. Even though this wasn't planned, throwing Kai under the bus for something he didn't do might be another way for me to get kicked out of here.

The teacher's face softens as much as it can, though it still looks like she's swallowed something bitter. "Oh, you poor thing. I'll take you to your class right away. The rest of you, good work, but it's time to get back to class now, all right?"

The three of them mutter their agreement in a distracted sort of way. All eyes are on me as I follow the teacher so she can show me the way. Before I get a chance to walk away, Emerson calls my name quietly.

When I look at her, that playful smirk creates a shining mischief in her brown eyes. "See you tomorrow," she says.

Then she walks away.

CHAPTER FIVE

I'm first to get to Kai's car when school is over. I lean against it with a long sigh, thinking about the past eight hours, wondering how on earth I've been going to school for so many years, how I'm capable of doing this every day. After gym, everything was boring and long. By last period, I was so bored out of my mind I got a bathroom pass and walked around again so I didn't have to listen to the art teacher talk about drawing for another second. Not to mention the fact both Emerson *and* Luke are in that class. Neither of them even looked at me the whole period, which I found just a tad strange, but wasn't the part that irked me so much. It was their constant joking and blatant disrespect for the teacher and other students. I get it, I'm hardly a star student, but the whole group of them was just too much for me. They were loud and obnoxious and downright ridiculous. I was relieved when the final bell rang and practically sprinted to the parking lot.

As I wait for Kai to get here, I admire all of the other seniors running to their own cars. I can't wait to be a senior in two years so I can actually see the light at the end of the tunnel, even if my personal light is dim and flickering.

"Oh, great. You're already here," I hear from behind me, and I turn to see Kai approaching. He looks angry.

"What's your problem?" I ask, not really caring much about the answer.

Kai laughs bitterly. "My problem. Well, maybe it's I got a C on my essay. Or I tripped on the stairs today. Or... hm... it's probably for my entire time in school, from Kindergarten until today, I've *never* been called to the principal's office. Until *you* show up."

I laugh uncertainly, wondering what sort of joke he's telling. "What are you talking about?"

"Oh, so you don't know? Or are you just lying again? You seem to love that."

My eyebrows raise. "Excuse me?"

Finally, he snaps, and I flinch a bit. "I was called out of class today because someone accused me of *bullying*. I get to the principal's office and she's already called my mother to ask her if there are problems at home. Which, of course, there very well might be now. The guidance counselor decided I'm suffering from *jealousy* and trying to lash out. All because you told some teacher I refused to show you how to get to class and you supposedly got lost."

I feel my heart sink to the ground. I cross my arms over my chest so he can't hear it.

"I didn't know they'd do that," I say indifferently. "But maybe you needed that. You know, to get some bad boy experience in before you finish up here."

Kai sighs loudly and opens his car door. I follow suit and get in, tossing my ratty backpack into the back seat noisily.

He puts the key into the ignition and takes a deep breath once more. "Lavender, I'm sorry you felt like you couldn't ask for help this morning and you felt like *you* had to lash out, but this isn't going to work if you don't—"

"Really, Kai? Are you *serious*? I just sent you to the principal's office for something you definitely didn't do and you're still trying to get me to like you? You're acting pathetic."

He looks at me with genuine surprise. "You think I want *you* to like me? I don't care what you think of me. But having you around means the world to the rest of my family, and if I have to be nice and respectful to you for you to stick around, so be it."

Looking him in the eyes, I realize *I'm* the pathetic one, acting out because people are treating me *too nicely.* But it can't be normal they're treating me like this. I just know it's some weird tactic to get me under control, and I won't comply. I won't.

"Fine, Kai. I'm sorry for ruining your perfect education with a little chat with the principal. I'm sure Harvard will let it slide."

Kai shakes his head, looking tired. Exhausted, even. He shifts the car into reverse. "You have no idea what you're talking about. If it makes you feel better to make assumptions about me and my family, whatever. But please, at the very least, pretend to be nice."

I sit back in my seat grumpily and look out the window. It's gloomy and gray outside and I'd love it if I weren't so frustrated. Everything is different here and I can't stand it. Why can't it just be normal? Why can't my foster parents be monstrous creatures who guard their refrigerator so I can't steal food? Or why can't the principal be some witch who tells me not to cause any trouble at her school, which could easily pass for a dungeon?

There's something weird going on here, and as the moments pass, I want to get out more and more. I'm beginning to wonder why my social worker ever thought this was a positive environment for me to live in. These people are *strange*.

We're quiet for the ride. Kai's music fills the space of the car, soothing and calm. I like what he's playing, but I wish I could listen to my own music. I could fall asleep to Kai's, but I would much rather enjoy something a little more upbeat right now. It would make everything more bearable. I have no headphones, though, and it isn't anything I'd create an issue out of.

So I enjoy Kai's music, whatever it is, and let my thoughts wander.

When we pull into the driveway, I let Kai go in through the front door first. I've never felt comfortable letting myself into any house since it isn't really mine. I feel even more uncomfortable knowing Kai hates me now.

I go right up to my room and toss my stuff on the floor before changing out of my baggy jeans and exchanging them for even baggier sweatpants. I got them from a thrift store a few months ago with the skimpy allowance my previous foster mother gave me.

When I collapse into bed, I almost immediately doze off, but my sleep is dreamless and black and seems to last only a few seconds.

I wake to some gentle knocking on my door.

Instead of getting up, I yell for the person to come in. Elise lets herself in quietly, shutting the door behind her.

"Sorry to wake you," she says softly, walking toward my bed.

"It's fine." I sit up and rub at my eyes, stifling a yawn.

She sits next to me on my bed. I notice she's still wearing her work clothes—some dress pants and a black, polka-dotted blouse—so maybe she's just gotten home. I haven't a clue what time it is, however.

"I just wanted to let you know dinner is ready," she says quietly, then hesitates. "And, well... I wanted to talk to you privately before we go downstairs."

I take a deep breath and give her an expectant look, waiting for her to go on.

Maybe I've already done it. My heart skips a beat in response. *Maybe she's already sick of me.*

She smiles at me tensely, her fingers fidgeting. "The school called me today. It seems like you had a rough first day. Do you want to talk about that?"

My excitement drops. I can think of roughly five thousand things I'd prefer to talk about. "No."

She nods as if she'd expected that response. "Okay. Well, I'll talk, then. I know you mentioned to the school Kai didn't give you the attention you needed today, and he will apologize as soon as you go downstairs. But I want to get to the bottom of why you felt you needed to go to the school for help. I want you to know you can come to us whenever you need. In fact, I've written out all our numbers, and I want you to put them into your phone right now so I know you have access to them."

I roll my eyes so I know she can see. This has got to be something new. The gentle tones, the walking on eggshells. It all feels like a little too much. But, still, I grab my phone from the bedside table as Elise pulls out a small piece of paper from her pocket. I read it, then transcribe each number into my phone.

When I'm finished, I say, "I didn't report anything. I told a teacher I got lost because I didn't want to get in trouble for being out of class. I didn't know they would call Kai to the office, okay?"

Elise looks concerned. "Why weren't you in class? Because you were lost, right?"

I laugh bitterly. "Yeah. Right. I was lost."

She looks away, and I can't tell what she's thinking. I *can* tell she probably isn't used to dealing with children who don't listen or act out for no reason. She definitely has no idea what to do with me, which is yet another reason why I have to get out of here.

Gently, she reiterates, "Like I said, dinner's ready, so let's head downstairs. All right?"

I nod once. "Yeah, sure."

I follow Elise out of the bedroom and downstairs. Kai, Leia, and Drew are already settled in at the dinner table, but none of them are eating just yet. Drew sees us first, and his face lights up immediately. He gives me a friendly greeting I do not return. I've been having trouble figuring that guy out. It was quickly established from the beginning he is clearly not the head of the house which is why I've homed in on Elise. I know she'll make the difference between my staying or going. But I haven't been in many houses where the mother is dominant. Drew seems to let Elise take the reins on all things parenting. He's reserved and quiet and, quite frankly, reminds me of Leia. He hasn't been causing me many issues, and neither has she.

Let's hope that doesn't change anytime soon.

Sitting down, I take in the meal before me. Chicken, rice, salad. Pretty standard meal, but something about it seems homier than ever. It's fragrant and steaming hot, colorful and even laid out nice. I hate that I'm starving and I'll love this food and I want to be sitting at this table right now. It would be so much easier if it was disgusting.

After everyone is served and has started eating, I watch as Elise looks to Kai and gestures for him to say something. He looks a little embarrassed and hesitant, which causes Elise to say his name in a slightly warning tone.

He puts his fork down and looks at me across the table. I am caught off guard with a mouthful of garlicky rice.

"Lavender, I am genuinely sorry for everything that happened today."

"What?" I stammer around the food. "But you already said before you—"

He goes on as if I haven't said anything. "I didn't mean to make you upset, and I take full responsibility for that."

I swallow, then respond, "Kai, you already said you're sorry, and you have no reason to be apologizing to me."

He doesn't say anything, just stares at his plate and picks his fork back up. But then he gives his mom a look, and I get angry.

"You actually forced him to say that, didn't you?" I scoff when no one says anything. "What, did you give him a *script*? Do you know how embarrassing it is you're taking advantage of your own son because he wants you to like him so bad?"

Everyone looks equally shocked and confused by my words, and I don't really know where they come from. I know I'm being unfair. I hardly know these people, but it *is* a little pathetic how obvious it is Elise made him say that. For some weird reason, they want me to like being here so bad, they're putting their children in uncomfortable situations on my behalf. I wonder if Leia's next, if she'll offer to hold my hand through dinner or something.

"Lavender, I have no idea what you're talking about," Elise says calmly. "That isn't the case at all. I just felt like Kai held a bit of responsibility for what happened today, and you deserved an apology."

I laugh loudly. "You have no idea what even happened today! You think the *principal* gave you an accurate account? You're *way* off. And you don't even care if Kai's innocent, you'll blame him just to make *me*, someone who isn't even a part of your family, feel better. Not to mention I literally suck."

I can't say I intentionally spewed all of that information out at them, and I bite my tongue as soon as I've said enough. Even so, I can tell I've had a wonderful effect on everyone. There is a simmering anger running throughout each of them, and I haven't a clue as to what exactly that anger is stemming from, but it tells me I'm a step closer to making them hate me and sending me on my way.

"You don't even yell at me." I lean back in my chair. "I could tell your son to go fuck himself, and you'd—"

"Lavender, just because you insist on saying these things doesn't mean we're at all okay with it," Elise interrupts. Magically, her voice is still steady, still calm. Unbelievable.

"So why don't you just get rid of me, then?"

I know from Elise's expression I've said the wrong thing. Her mouth drops open for a moment as she sits completely still, flabbergasted. She finally shakes her head, almost as if to bring herself back. Still, she can hardly get her words out. "Get rid of you? Is that what this is about? You're afraid we're going to get rid of you?"

I look at the ceiling, shaking my head. I don't say anything.

"We aren't planning on giving up on you anytime soon, honey. That isn't the type of people we are, none of us. We want to help you. We know you've been through quite a lot, and I know we haven't been the best support system so far, but we're learning. We just need your help back, is all."

The way she says it makes it seem like she's genuine, but is she? Maybe what she's saying really just means she's going to fix me, as I've been speculating. Maybe these people don't even realize the difference between helping and fixing me. No, they clearly don't, because if they actually wanted to help me, they'd leave me alone. They'd leave me alone and mind their own business.

"Fine," is all I say though. "Whatever."

After that, dinner is scarily silent.

I'm good at quieting a room. Not such a bad talent, right?

CHAPTER SIX

The following days are equally as quiet. It's almost eerie. I can tell the Kahales are trying their best to stay out of my business, but that doesn't keep them from asking me every night to watch TV with them. It doesn't stop them all, even Kai, from being overly nice to me. Kai doesn't show any signs he's mad at me anymore, which honestly just seems fake, but it doesn't matter.

Even so, I avoid them all for whole days if possible. My bedroom has become the only place I feel any semblance of comfort, and even there I feel out of place because it isn't really *mine*. I'm cold and distant at dinner, but I've found it difficult to purposely act up to forward my plan of getting kicked out, simply because it's tiring. It requires effort and thought to speak out of turn, to run late in the mornings. Not only that, but I hardly get responses, and I'm starting to think my efforts might not be getting me anywhere. Nevertheless, I plan on continuing, even if I'm dead tired at bedtime.

The more tired and stressed I've been getting, the more I tic. I've always had these tics in my face, ankles, wrists, and while breathing, but in the past couple of days, it's gotten a lot worse. I have no idea why or how to fix it, and trying to mask it in public to prevent humiliation is growing nearly impossible, so whenever I get back to the house and in my bedroom, I find myself screaming into my pillow out of pure frustration.

School itself is a complete haze. Sometimes I'm so aware of my tics or breathing I block out whole classes and walk out after what feels like mere seconds of sitting down. The only good thing about being me is teachers tend to be a little understanding, but I will say at Springfield, the teachers expect so much of me. It's just another one of those weird things about this town to add to the list. After almost every class, the teacher will pull me to the side to have a discussion about my work, my concentration levels, my concerns, *their* concerns. It's draining. And how do I explain to a teacher who genuinely wants me to do well I'm a natural-born underachiever? It's impossible.

I'm grateful for the break a Friday promises when it comes. The thought of sleeping in on Saturday morning sounds absolutely splendid, and I have a feeling the Kahales will let me do it. They haven't provided me with chores or anything thus far, which is what I would typically do on a Saturday morning at other houses. I'm planning on sleeping until noon, which is a rarity in my life.

The school day is halfway over and I'm walking through the crowded hall thinking about my sleeping plans, when I accidentally bump into someone walking in the opposite direction. I look back, about to apologize, but I see who it is.

Emerson.

She, of course, looks flawless. Her hair falls in its natural waves to just past her shoulders. Her skin is perfectly clear, glowing even under fluorescent lights. She wears a pink plaid skirt and an oversized white sweater that swallows her whole. I can't say why, but I hate she looks so good. Not hate; *despise*.

And from the look on her face, she definitely bumped into me on purpose.

"Really?" I snap, turning fully.

Emerson giggles. "A little cranky today, are we?"

Instinctively, my arms cross over my chest. "Why would you care, little miss perfect? Haven't you ever been cranky before?"

For a moment it looks like I've hurt her, really, but the moment passes in an instant. Coolly, Emerson continues. "Don't take it out on me." A knowing smirk creeps onto her lips. "It's not my fault you have a crush on me."

"*What*?" I exclaim, physically stepping back. Who does she think she is, making that kind of assumption?

Emerson laughs hysterically, her eyes cast up to the ceiling, horribly adorable. Ugh.

"You heard me! The whole 'being mean to your crush' trope is so outdated and sexist. Not to mention *boring*."

I scoff angrily. "I have no idea what you're talking about. That's *ridiculous*."

Emerson raises her perfectly-shaped eyebrows suggestively. I shake my head, frustrated, but the smile on her face only grows wider, reaching her big brown eyes playfully. I turn stiffly, ignoring the heat in my cheeks and listening to her laugh fade as I walk away in a rush.

It plays in my head for the rest of the day.

* * *

When I get into art, I'm relieved we're working individually. The teacher lets us use headphones to listen to music, and I asked Kai this morning if I could borrow his. I know it was a low thing to do, but it's only for today. I promised not only him, but myself as well. I wouldn't take advantage of this sort of thing and end up relying on him.

I settle on the uncomfortable, freezing cold metal stool, putting my bag down after getting out my materials, including my phone and Kai's headphones. I wait for the teacher to give an introduction to class after the bell rings. She likes for us to listen first, and then we're off to do our own thing.

Mrs. Nortan introduces the class by re-explaining the assignment, which is an abstract drawing technique we learned yesterday. After, she tells us to get to work, and I put in the headphones excitedly, opting for something soft but alternative. Grabbing a ruler, I start tracing lines onto the paper provided, eventually becoming engrossed in my project, the class fading away around me.

The project may be busywork, but it's become something I look forward to daily now. I like the freedom of it, the fact we could choose our own colors and design, but what I like even better is there's practically no way to do it wrong since it's abstract. I choose the primary colors—red, yellow, and blue—and outline the shapes in a thick, black line.

I haven't a clue as to how much time has passed when I feel a tap on my shoulder, but by then, all my red shapes are finished and I've moved onto blue. I turn around immediately, thinking it's the teacher, and take my headphones out.

For the second time today, I am surprised to see Emerson standing in front of me.

It is, perhaps, more unusual for her to purposely seek me out. She typically doesn't even *look* at me in this class. Here, we are two completely different species on two completely separate planets. Forget planets, *dimensions.* When Emerson's friends are around, she couldn't care less about bothering me, I've noticed. For this, I am grateful, but today it seems her friends can't protect me from interaction.

As it turns out, a quick glance around the room tells me her friends are nowhere to be found. It clicks why she'd be so interested in bothering me.

"What do you want?" I ask with exasperation, turning back to my work.

Emerson laughs lightly. "You really *aren't* having a good day, are you?"

I ignore this. "Emerson, what do you want from me?"

I look away from her as she decides to take a seat next to me. I try focusing even harder on my work, but for some reason, I feel pressured with someone watching me.

"I have something for you," she says to me, and I furrow my brow in response. "Here."

She hands me a folded slip of paper.

"What is this?"

That smile returns to her face. Or maybe it never left. All she seems to do is smile. How could someone be so happy all the time, or even compelled to smile so much? Don't her cheeks hurt? I'm exhausted just looking at it.

"It's my number."

I unfold the slip and see it is, in fact, her number, or *a* number at least. For all I know, this could be a prank, but I don't let that intrusive thought take over just yet. Instead, I look between her and the paper blankly.

"Why would I want or need this?" I deadpan.

She shrugs lightheartedly, but she doesn't look me in the eye when she replies, and when she does it is in a softer, but still playful, tone. "I figured I'd make the first move in case you were too scared. You know, it's okay you have a crush on me."

Is she serious? Why does she think I have a crush on her? Have I given off some sign I do? Because I definitely don't, and she is *way* off here.

"I most certainly do *not* have a crush on you."

Her knowing look terrifies me for reasons I cannot explain. She says, "Okay," sarcastically before walking away as her friends parade back into the classroom. I shove the piece of paper into my backpack without looking at it, just so I don't hurt her feelings.

CHAPTER SEVEN

After school, I head straight to the bedroom like always. Kai doesn't try to stop me. I still have no idea what time everyone else comes home since I'm holed up in my room every day until dinner. I don't particularly care what time that is, but it does occur to me I have truly put distance between myself and the Kahales in the way I intended. I try to pride myself on not giving them the chance to form a relationship with me, try to feel happy about it, but instead, I just feel exhausted.

Once in my bedroom, I change out of my school clothes, get under the thick, white covers, and fall asleep very quickly, eager to stop thinking about anything for a while. I'd been dreaming of this nap for hours. And since it's the weekend, I can sleep peacefully without worrying about homework or waking up early in the morning.

My sleep doesn't live up to my expectations, however. I have vivid, tense dreams I wake up from consistently. Whenever I pick up my head to look at the time, it's almost exactly two hours or so from the last time I checked. Even so, my tiredness does not deplete. Somehow, though, my energy does. So I keep on sleeping, trying desperately to chase away the feeling of emptiness that resides in my body.

I end up dozing right through dinner and waking up with a start at ten o'clock at night. I'd been dreaming about walking through a dark forest shrouded in darkness and jolted awake when some shadow pounced at me from behind a twisting tree.

I shoot out of bed, feeling oddly guilty and unsettled. I wonder if Elise came in and saw me sleeping or if she just knocked and knocked before eventually giving up and going back downstairs. They were all probably relieved they could have a normal family dinner tonight. Without me there, I'm sure it was more pleasant. They could talk, be themselves. They didn't have to walk on eggshells. I already know I've created an uncomfortable environment in their home without realizing my actions had this consequence. It makes me feel worse than I'd care to admit. The rising dread leads me out of my room and straight to the bathroom, where I run the cold water and splash it frantically against my hot cheeks.

Staring at myself in the mirror, I take in my wildly tousled blond hair that is knotted in the ponytail I put it in this morning. My chin drips with tap water as I stare into my own dark eyes, my chest rising and falling with breaths I'm starting to feel like I don't deserve.

What kind of person am I, to come into the home of a family who took me in, only to drive them away from me? And in the process, drive them away from each other?

I know why. I know why I have to do this. But this selfishness feels foreign to me for the first time in so long. I'd grown accustomed to doing things for my own safety and benefit. No one else has ever looked out for me, so I learned to do it myself.

But this... this might be my worst endeavor yet.

Fine, that little voice in my brain says. *Let them take advantage of you. Let them manipulate you. Let them control you.*

I'm so conflicted with what my brain is telling me because it doesn't feel like anyone is taking advantage of me. I know I have to take care of myself, though. No one else is going to do it. So I'll keep doing this, whatever *this* is, and eventually I won't feel so bad anymore. Because eventually, I'll understand what exactly they're trying to do to me and what I'm doing won't seem nearly as horrible.

I'm interrupted by a ravenous growl in my stomach. I look down as if there will be a monster waiting to greet me, but, no. I'm just starving since I missed dinner.

I've never done it before, but I wonder if I can go get something from the kitchen by myself. I never ask foster families for food or anything, but the Kahales are different. Even if I *do* get in trouble, I'm sure it will only speed up my exit out of here.

This thought sends me on my way downstairs.

Once I'm downstairs, I hear the television quietly playing. When I get into the living room, I can't see anyone's head above the back of the couch, so I figure someone left it on. Most of the lights are off. The house is quiet and dim, filled with warmth. As I sneak closer to the kitchen, I jump when I notice Leia curled up under a plaid blanket next to Hiro on the couch, who sleeps soundly on his back, paws up in the air shamelessly.

I debate going back up, but Leia sees me before I can make a move.

"Oh," she exclaims softly. "I'm sorry, I didn't hear you coming. Do you want me to leave?"

"What?" I ask, surprised. "Of course not. I just... well, I missed dinner, and I was wondering if I could get something to eat."

"Yeah, of course," Leia responds, sitting up. "We had Chinese food. There are some leftovers in the fridge if you want. I'll show you how to use the microwave."

I'm already shaking my head. "No, no, I can eat it cold. It's okay."

But she's already getting up, a small smile on her lips. "It's no big deal. I'll show you and you can use it whenever you want."

"Oh... um, okay. That sounds fine."

I let her lead me to the kitchen. She flicks on an overhead light that makes me squint. From the stainless steel fridge, Leia takes out white containers filled with food and sets them on the counter. She tells me to take as much as I want, and I do with the silverware she gives me. Once I've filled my plate, she sets my dish in the microwave and goes about putting the food back where it was.

I know this is a simple, perhaps unnecessary act, but it makes my heart flood with joy. Sure, I could've easily eaten the food cold or even figured out the microwave on my own. Instead, Leia has gone out of her way to do something genuinely kind. I don't know if I expected anything else from her, really; she's so timid and sweet all of the time, this is probably light work for her.

But Leia and I haven't ever *really* spoken. I purposely try to avoid her *because* she's so sweet and kind. Most importantly, she's innocent in this situation. She has had no part in getting me here and has had no part in treating me differently. She's just been there, always quiet, but always watching, too. I think she's a good person, and I don't want to hurt her.

I also think she wants a sister, and I am certainly not that person, so it's best I keep away from her.

When the microwave goes off, Leia hands me the plate and asks if I want to sit on the couch with her and watch television. I'm immediately about to say no, but I think about sitting in the bedroom alone again and find myself saying yes. There's no harm in one night. Right?

We settle in around Hiro, who only stirs to smell my food. After deciding it isn't worth it, he plops right back down and falls asleep almost instantly, snoring loudly.

Leia plays her show, and I have no idea what show it is or what's happening in it. All I really pick up on is bright neon lights and some synth soundtrack music that catches my attention. Leia is completely engaged in it. She has that concentrated but distant look on her face most people do when they're watching their favorite show, all comfortable on their couch at home. My mind begins to wander as I search her focused stare.

I've been at this house a week and have never sat on this couch. I've never sat this close to the cat or Leia. It's just... weird. Maybe not weird, but new. I can't decide how I truly feel about it. Instead of trying, I focus wholly on eating my food, which is actually really good.

A few minutes go by, and I'm still invested in my food. I don't notice Leia staring at me until she says something.

"You don't like staying here, right?" she asks, and I'm once again caught off guard by her.

I hesitate. I don't know how to explain it without sounding crazy. "I don't like staying anywhere. It isn't your fault."

She looks incredibly young with her hair down and her baggy t-shirt on. I know she's in seventh grade, but for a moment she seems so small. "But why? Why don't you like staying anywhere?"

I shrug and put my plate down on the coffee table. "I've never had a home. I don't like other people's."

Leia looks thoughtfully at the blanket on her lap and plays with loose threads on it. Her brow is furrowed deeply. "I can't imagine not having a home. I'm sorry."

All of a sudden, I feel like crying, but I swallow hard to make it go away. I sigh. "You don't have to be sorry. Like I said, it isn't your fault."

"I know it isn't my fault, but... it makes me sad. I wish... I don't know."

She looks nervous, fumbly, and clearly doesn't want to finish her sentence, but I'm curious to know what she wishes, so I ask, "You wish what?"

Leia looks up at me, her gaze clear and focused now. "I wish this could be your home. But I know you don't like it. So I at least hope you can find a home, even if it isn't here."

I look away from her so she doesn't notice she's struck something inside of me that threatens to pour out. "Well, thank you. No one's ever said anything like that to me before."

We sit in silence for a few moments, staring at our laps and wondering if we should drop the conversation.

But Leia picks it up again and timidly asks me, "Do you ever feel really anxious? Or nervous?"

The question confuses me, but I respond, "I always feel anxious. My social worker once told me I probably have an anxiety disorder, but I never went to a doctor, so I don't know. Why do you ask?"

Leia looks nervous right now, actually, like she wishes she never spoke. "No reason. I-I feel like that, too, sometimes. I don't know why I asked."

She offers me a soft smile, clearly wanting to drop the conversation. Her hand moves absently to Hiro's plush fur, who makes a sound of protest at the disruption to his precious sleep. Leia and I laugh quietly together.

After our shared moment, we silently decide to go back to watching television, but something's changed between us and I know we're both aware of it. I was so distant from her before for so many reasons, and it wasn't so scary getting to know her a little just now. But what happens when I have to leave? Already, the thought of leaving her behind makes my chest hurt, but I try to remind myself why this is necessary. Sure, Leia is probably great to be around, but other, more important aspects of this placement aren't working for me, which means I can't stay.

But despite my constant self-reassurance, there has been a permanent doubt placed in my brain. And no matter what I do, it is stubborn.

* * *

The next morning, I am wide awake. I anxiously await the wan autumn light, hoping it will fill the room with some warmth so I can move from my frozen place on the bed and think of anything else besides last night.

I didn't sleep another wink after talking with Leia.

It was around midnight when she decided she was tired. I pretended I was as well and came to the bedroom, but as soon as I laid in the bed, monsters filled my brain to the brim.

It started with overthinking, led to intrusive thoughts, and by the end of it, I was convinced if I stayed in this place a second longer, I'd die. I know I won't, but it took me a while to convince myself it was all in my head.

I've never been this confused about a placement before. At the beginning of my journey in the foster care system, I was too young to even know what was happening. At age three, I was probably content with anyone giving me attention and food. I don't remember much from when I was that young. Mostly I just remember flashes of color and the faces of strangers.

Once I was older, about six or seven, I anticipated every new home would be a fresh start, with new memories and a new environment. Every time I held out hope I was one day going to find a mom, dad, sister, or brother. But I got used to the foul treatment of money-hungry foster parents who didn't care about my well-being past ensuring I was alive and breathing.

I eventually got used to this and stopped feeling any sense of anticipation. I came to the stark conclusion at age twelve nowhere would ever feel perfect because no home belonged to me. Kids who found their "forever homes" were either myths or rarities. It made me upset and frustrated, which probably made my foster parents doubly upset and frustrated. Once I was used to the way the system worked, I wasn't concerned about finding that nurturing environment I longed for at the start. I was concerned only with getting out of the foster system at eighteen.

Living here is making me question that safety spot I settled in four years ago. My end goal will always be to get out of the system and be on my own, but this environment is not something I'm used to. If it is, in fact, what I think, they're attempting to fix me, to control me, but in a different way. I need to get back to what I'm used to. I need to stay sane until I can try to live life on my own. But if not, if this is real…

I can't let my thoughts run past that. I can't. It isn't true. I still have to get out of here. I'm sure of it.

It takes loads of self-control to wait until I hear movement coming from downstairs to go down there. No matter what happened with Leia last night, I will never feel comfortable walking through a house like it's mine. I only did it yesterday because I was desperate.

But when I hear dishes clanking and quiet voices, I dash out of my room at the speed of light, down the stairs and into the kitchen.

"Oh, good morning, Lavender," Elise states, chipper as ever. "How did you sleep?"

"Fine," I say grumpily. "Are we having breakfast?"

Elise laughs lightly. "Hungry from last night, is that right?"

"Yeah, I—"

"I gave Lavender some leftovers last night," Leia interjects, and I look at her in a panic. Is she trying to get me in trouble?

"Oh, you did?" Elise asks. "That's great, I'm glad you had a chance to eat! I was worried about you."

I'm shocked by her response until I remind myself this isn't a normal foster family. Of course, she doesn't care I ate their leftovers without permission.

"Yeah, uh... it was good. Thanks."

Elise nods. Drew walks in just then, saying, "Whose having pancakes?"

Leia and Kai both exclaim, "Me!" and though I'm starving and definitely about to eat tons of pancakes, I don't say anything.

I'm about to sit when Elise comes up to me. She pulls her fluffy blue robe tightly around herself and gives me a gentle smile.

"Can I speak to you privately for a minute, please?" she asks kindly enough, though I feel my heart pounding in my chest.

I nod stiffly and follow her into the living room, which is hardly private from the kitchen, but still away from the others. Every *second* I'm being caught off guard by these people.

She sits on the couch and I do too, waiting for whatever she's going to say. I feel my sweaty hands ball into fists in my lap and let my mind run through intrusive thought after intrusive thought. Sure, this might be what I want—to get in trouble, to get kicked out—but that doesn't make getting yelled at any easier.

"How are you feeling?" she inquires, sounding sincere. Even the way she furrows her brow over her mug of coffee makes her seem genuine.

"Fine. Why?" I respond dryly.

Hesitating, she readjusts herself on the couch. "We've all noticed you have been having trouble adjusting, Lavender, and I think going to see a therapist might be a good idea."

The anger creeps in unexpectedly. It almost feels familiar in my body because of the calm numbness that has swept over me the past couple of days. It takes a few moments for Elise's words to truly seep in.

But she continues.

"I know a really great counseling service that was recommended to me by a coworker of mine, and I really think if you give it a chance, you'll—"

"I'll *what*? Be a good little girl? Be compliant? Do chores for you? Whatever it is, I want nothing to do with it," I spit. My voice raises slightly, and I can tell everyone in the kitchen is trying hard not to listen.

Elise looks taken aback. "That isn't at all what I meant, Lavender. I care about *you*. I want you to feel better, to do better."

"But you don't know anything about me! How could you make all these assumptions about my mental health without even *asking* me?"

Calmly, Elise responds, "When I try to talk to you, we fight, and on account I'm in charge here, I think this is the best course of action—"

"You're in *charge*," I scoff, spreading my hands. "Yeah, no kidding. You *are* in charge. So what are you gonna do? Drag me there? Because it's a little embarrassing you'd drag *me* there when your own daughter is suffering before your eyes and you don't do anything about it!"

At this point, I'm yelling, and everyone hears. Including Leia. The heat in my cheeks is both anger and embarrassment. I wish I could take it back. *I wish I could take it back.*

For the first time, I watch as anger rises in Elise, her jaw noticeably clenching and her eyes narrowing. I am terrified of what she could possibly say, but it's worse than anything I would've imagined.

"In the same way I don't know a thing about you, Lavender, you wouldn't know the first thing about my family since you don't *care* enough to know," she reprimands, pointing a finger at me. She seems to notice this and crosses her arms instead. In a more reserved, but equally as firm, tone, she continues, "You have no right to speak to me about *my daughter*, whom you also know absolutely nothing about. What's embarrassing is you'd think saying something that hurtful would be okay, especially in front of Leia."

"You're right, I don't care!" I stand up, letting the hurt and pain turn into sheer rage. It's better this way. It has to be. "I don't care about you or your family or your idiotic counseling services because I will never see you again when I'm out of here, so why try?" I look at them all standing in the kitchen, at their nearly identical expressions filled with disappointment. My voice fades with my failing energy. "Why even fucking try?"

I storm away, my feet pounding the floor excessively, but again, I don't care. Elise is right about everything and I hate her and I hate she's right. I simply hate it. This is toxic for me. All I do is fight with her over nonsense. At other foster homes, I was yelled at, but at least it was because I did something wrong. I tossed a red shirt in a white wash, I accidentally spilled bleach on the carpet, I put too much salt in the pasta. But what did I do? What did I *really* do?

When I reach the bedroom, I slam the door so hard I'm surprised the house doesn't shake. I collapse into the bed, the tears already flowing, and I scream into my pillow. Loud. Louder. Until I can't breathe. Why is this so hard?

I cry until I can't anymore.

CHAPTER EIGHT

My vision is gray and blurry on Sunday morning. I didn't sleep at all. I feel sick and past the point of exhaustion. I made a mistake. Elise made a mistake, too, but it was my fault. Everything is my fault. After all, if I hadn't showed up here, none of this would have ever happened. To them or me.

I suck.

I'm hesitant to leave my room even when I hear people walking around downstairs. I did not come out for dinner last night. I waited until I was sure everyone was asleep, including Leia, and snuck up some snacks to my room. I didn't enjoy any part of it, but I knew I needed to eat. It wasn't enough, however. I'm starving again this morning, and I don't know what to do about it.

I'm ashamed of myself and embarrassed to see any of the Kahales, specifically Elise and Leia. I made a fool of myself yesterday morning after having a genuinely positive moment with Leia. I don't think I've ever had a positive moment with anyone in my entire life, and of course, I screwed up the first and only one ever.

In the end, my stomach drives me straight downstairs, as per usual. As soon as I smell eggs and bacon, I know I made the right decision, despite the awkward encounters that are sure to ensue my arrival.

Everyone is already sitting at the table, eating, smiling, and talking. It all stops when they see me. Even Leia avoids my eyes, though she greeted me with a smile and a wave every morning the past week.

"I'm sorry, but I'm really hungry. I can take my food up to my room if you'd prefer that," I say timidly.

Elise shakes her head. "Of course not. You can eat with us. You're always welcome to. I think we have to talk, anyway."

"Uh... okay." I nod slowly and make my way to the cupboard to grab a plate. The feeling is unnatural, but I can't say doing something so simply independent doesn't fill me with a thrill.

I scoop scrambled eggs and bacon onto my plate, then take out silverware for myself. Making my way to the table, I set my things down and take a seat, glancing around awkwardly.

"Lavender, I want to start out by saying I will never raise my voice like that again. I apologize to not only you, but also to you two." She gestures to Kai and Leia. "Because I know you've never really had to see me raise my voice like that. And to you, Lavender, I hope you know that isn't who I am. That isn't who we are." She looks at Drew, who nods his head solemnly.

"Both of us grew up with parents who would yell at us to solve problems," Drew explains. "It was one of the reasons we got along so well when we first met. We understood the other's pain and mutually agreed we'd never raise children that way. Yelling and fighting fixes absolutely nothing."

Elise agrees. "It's my fault I let my anger get the best of me. Problems aren't solved with screaming, arguing. They're solved by talking. My idea of counseling was because of that.

I figured if you didn't want to talk to us, maybe you'd want to talk to a stranger. I apologize for making the wrong assumption. As for Leia, well…"

Elise looks at Leia and smiles warmly. Leia gives her a small one in return, then plays with her eggs with her fork.

"I spoke to Leia about this, and she said it was okay to tell you. We've been working on Leia's anxiety since we found out about it, but she's too nervous to see a therapist. We're working up to it. I'm sorry it seemed like we weren't doing enough for her to you. I assure you we're all trying our best here."

I look away, my appetite suddenly gone. The painful lump in my throat has returned, but I grit my teeth and will it away. This is no place to cry. I have no right to cry.

"I'm sorry, too," I say seriously. "I had no place in saying what I did. I didn't mean it."

Elise gives me a firm nod. "I'm glad we're able to talk through this. When we're both ready to, we should revisit talking about other things, but I know that isn't possible for right now, and that's okay. I just want you to know this is a communicative household, and it's okay to talk if you want to. All right?"

Nodding silently, I remember distantly I won't be here long enough to have that conversation, to feel what it's like to live in a communicative household, whatever that means. I appreciate the apology, but does that change the situation? Not really. Elise is still trying to put me in counseling to have some form of control over me. It's not that I'm not used to being controlled by adults, but I wish she'd make me wash the dishes or scrub the floors instead of trying to get inside my brain. Maybe it seems weird I'd want that, but at least it would be something familiar, something I could actually comply with.

The only problem now is it won't only hurt them if I lash out now. Because I've let myself feel for them, it'll hurt me, too.

* * *

Sleep does not find me easily that night, either. I only get a few hours in before my alarm blares and scares me awake. When it does, I groan loudly and almost feel like sobbing. I just want rest. I can already tell this day will be awful because of how hard it is for me to get out of bed.

Getting ready is difficult but quick, my muscles creaking with the effort to stand and operate. My body is heavy and sluggish, eyes watery and burning. When I'm ready, I head downstairs and prepare myself some toast while making stiff small talk with Leia. She tells me about her math test today and I tell her about my Spanish quiz on verb conjugation. I'm positive we couldn't have a drier conversation. I can't tell if it's me who drives this dryness or if it's her. Maybe it's both of us.

Kai comes downstairs soon after our conversation trickles away and asks me if I'm ready to head out. I pop the rest of the toast in my mouth, nodding, and walk outside.

The air is colder than usual today and smells of snow. It hasn't snowed yet this year, though I hope it will soon, and I think about it all the way to school. Kai plays soft indie music that makes me want to shut my eyes. Before I know it, we're in the school parking lot, and I'm dragging myself out of the car.

At the entrance, Kai and I say goodbye to each other so we can head to our respective classes; Kai heads to Calculus while I head to PE. I'm walking for only a few seconds when I'm approached by Luke, to my utter surprise.

"Hey, Lavender, how are you?" he asks, as if we're best friends. He joins me by my side, walking at my pace.

Dully, I respond, "What do you want?"

Luke looks hurt. "What happened to *hello*? How are you? How was your week—"

"You don't talk to me, so I know you want something. What is it? Do I need to vote for you to be president of the school? Homecoming king? Biggest idiot?"

His eyebrows shoot up, and he moves in front of me so we both stop walking. "I'm highly offended by that."

I smile sweetly. "Good."

"I only wanted to talk to you about Emerson."

I furrow my brow. "Emerson? What about her?"

Luke shrugs and leans against the wall. "She didn't come to school today. She's been sulking because you haven't called or texted her."

Scoffing, I shake my head. "Emerson is missing a day of school because I haven't texted her? No way in hell."

Luke hesitates. "Well, I actually have no idea why she didn't come today. She wouldn't tell me. The thing about her sulking is unrelated."

I spread my hands, looking at him expectantly. "So? Why are you telling me this?"

"Well, she'd kill me if she knew I said this, but she's serious about liking you. The only reason I'm actually saying anything is because she thinks you hate her, which I know isn't true, and I'm tired of seeing Emerson sad all the time."

"What does this have to do with me?" I say, trying to ignore the flutter in my stomach. My hands clench by my sides as my tics act up with the stress of the situation. There's no way Emerson actually likes *me*, but I have to keep it cool so Luke doesn't see me getting flustered over it. "I get it, she has a crush or whatever, but what do you want me to do about it? Neither of you really know me, and I won't be here much longer, so it's probably best both of you stay away from me."

Luke looks at me skeptically, standing upright. "What's that supposed to mean?"

"It means exactly what I said. Now, I'm sorry, but I have to get to class."

I walk away before he can say anything. I know it isn't certain when I'll be leaving here, but it's probably best Emerson takes her eyes off of me, if that's really what's going on here. I doubt she actually likes me. She probably just wants me to vote for *her* to be homecoming queen or something.

* * *

Unfortunately, the day does not improve. I bomb my Spanish quiz so hard the teacher immediately asks to see me after class. Luke stares at me for all of art class, trying to telepathically tell me to call Emerson or something. And when I get in the car with Kai, he's acting *really* weird. Whenever he looks at me, it's with pity and caution, which isn't unusual from anybody when they're around me, but I thought I was past that with Kai. I guess not, but it makes me uncomfortable.

When we pull into the driveway, though, I know I'm missing something. I haven't picked up on *much* here, but I know for a fact there shouldn't be any cars in the driveway since both Elise and Drew work late. Today, both of their cars are there.

"Why are your parents home?" I ask Kai casually.

He shrugs, not looking at me. "I guess you'll find out."

Widening my eyes, I undo my seatbelt and grab my backpack from the backseat. We get out of the car, and Kai purposely lets me walk in front of him, as if I'm about to walk into a deep, dark cave with no end in sight.

"What's wrong with you, Kai?" I ask as I open the door.

He doesn't answer. Because waiting by the door are Drew and Elise, looking nervous and anxious. Their heads pop up at the sight of me, and they rush to me silently.

"Are you okay?" Elise asks me hurriedly.

"What? I'm fine, why?"

Elise briefly looks at Kai, then back at me. The worried look only worsens, which concerns me. "Kai told us about how you're planning on trying to hurt yourself in some way, Lavender."

I look at Kai in disbelief, wondering what Elise could be talking about, but Kai won't make eye contact with me. Looking back at Elise, I ask, "What are you talking about?"

Elise takes a step toward me. She looks like she's fighting for composure, but I can't tell if she's fighting anger, sadness, something else. "Kai told us he'd heard you're going to try hurting yourself. Please don't be upset with him. We're all just looking out for you. We don't want you to do this to yourself. Whatever we can do to help you, please just tell us."

I try to gloss over the events of the day in my mind, but I keep coming up short. What could she be referring to?

Confusedly, I respond, "Elise, I'm sorry, but I literally have no idea what you're talking about."

Kai steps forward and finally looks at me. The look on his face is one of distress, almost misery. "I'm sorry, Lavender. Luke told me what you said to him, and I got really worried. I just didn't know who else to tell."

I narrow my eyes at Kai, though it isn't him I'm mad at. "What did *Luke* tell you?"

He suddenly looks unsure, as if maybe he did something wrong. "He told me you mentioned to him you... you weren't going to be here anymore, and you were going to try hurting yourself."

I scoff, scrubbing at my face with my hands. I feel cold laughter bubbling out of me for reasons I can't explain. "Luke's an idiot. That isn't what I told him *at all*."

I mean, I *did* tell him I'd be out of here soon, but I didn't mean it like that. Even so, the Kahales don't have to know what I actually meant.

"Luke keeps bothering me about this girl Emerson, and I told him I probably wouldn't be here long, anyway. So she shouldn't get attached to me in case I have to move foster homes. That was all I said, and the idiot thought I was about to off myself. How did he even gather that?"

I'm laughing hysterically, trying to imagine me making Luke all nervous and worried. I can't believe he went to Kai. And how could Kai go straight to his parents without even asking me about it first?

As soon as I think about it, I realize he's probably got orders from his mom to send her updates about me or something. This entire family is most definitely consulting and conspiring about me behind my back. I mean, why wouldn't they? They had a perfectly normal family before I jumped into the mix. I'm honestly surprised they haven't tried removing me. Aren't they sick of me yet?

I definitely think I'm sick of them, and the fact I've been involved in so much drama after being here for only a week. I'm so used to sitting around at foster homes, minding my business, having just about no communication with anybody around me. That's what's normal to me. That's how I've been able to bear being in the system. I haven't been the most behaved, I'll admit, but that's just because foster homes can get toxic quickly.

Somehow, this has been toxic for me since the very beginning, and I can't pinpoint why.

It feels like I'm fighting with someone every day. Like I have to talk to people and keep up this pretense of being a productive member of society when, in reality, all I want to do is mind my business and ignore everybody. But because I haven't been able to do that, I've been exhausted. My body is sore, my tics are worsening by the day. I'm anxious all the time. I have nightmares, and even when I sleep for hours, I'm more tired after than before.

It has to be because of this environment, right? I'm not thriving here and it's affecting my health. That has to be it.

I've known I have to get out of here from the moment I walked in. But now I realize it has to be soon. Like, today.

It's no joke my mental health has been deteriorating from the moment I stepped foot in this place. Not only that, but the force of keeping myself away from Leia is so hard—it's becoming more and more apparent we'd get along, and I can't let that happen. It would be better if I was gone from here. Maybe my life won't be perfect somewhere else, but at least I'll be stable. At least I'll be somewhere I'm used to.

"Lavender?" Elise says cautiously. "Are you all right?"

I realize distantly I've zoned out a little bit and have not caught the last few things that were said.

"Yes," I say numbly. "I'm perfectly fine."

"So you're sure Luke made a mistake, right? You're not in any danger?" Kai asks me. He looks genuinely worried.

I give him a stiff smile and nod. I can't have them snooping around me at all hours of the day, so I may as well console them. "Luke made a mistake. I'm not gonna hurt myself, okay? I'm sorry you got involved in this, all of you."

Everyone looks relieved. Drew gives me an encouraging smile I do not return. My mind is whirring too loudly and quickly for me to focus on anything except getting out of here.

* * *

It's eleven o'clock at night when I stop hearing noise coming from the rest of the house. After dinner, I went straight up to my room to go to bed early, but instead of doing that, I packed up my clothes and school books, along with my meager supply of personal items—my phone, some toiletries, and my favorite book, which I "accidentally" stole from a library in the city.

For the past couple of hours, I've been sitting on my bed in the dark, letting my anxiety run through my veins, up and down, to the point where I am now shaking. These hours have felt like years. But I finally heard Kai brushing his teeth and making his way to his room for good, and now it's been a full forty-five minutes since I heard any noise. I'm grateful it's a school night, since that means everyone goes to bed a little earlier. I don't know how much longer I would've been able to sit here like this.

I get up from my bed silently and walk to my backpack, which rests against the wall in the corner of the bedroom. I put up my sweatshirt hood so my hair is covered, then swing my backpack on. Sighing, I look around at the room and feel an immense sense of dread.

I know it's just because I'm doing something risky and not because I'm leaving this room. I have no attachment to it. And this *is* risky. If I'd gotten kicked out, I would've headed straight to a group home, where I'd have my eighteenth and final birthday in foster care. But the repercussions for running away from a foster home are much, much worse. Every foster kid knows that. I feel trapped here, though, and I have no desire to go to a group home. If this works out, I won't have to stay here or go to a group home. I'll be *free*. The thought sends a spike of adrenaline through me I don't entirely like, but I have to pretend I'm excited despite the overbearing fear I will be caught. I won't be. I won't.

I open my bedroom door as quietly as possible and look around to make sure there's no one around. The hallway is pitch black, and I don't hear anybody. I tiptoe slowly and cautiously to the staircase. When I get there, I shine my phone's light on them so I don't fall. When I'm at the front door, I hesitate.

You have to do this, the voice in my head tells me. I take a few deep breaths and try to get the terror out of my body. It stays put.

Opening the door, I feel a gush of freezing cold wind blow my hair back. Swallowing thickly, I continue breathing deeply as I step outside into the cold, then shut the door as quietly as possible behind me.

With one final, deep breath, I begin to run.

CHAPTER NINE

After two minutes of running, I'm sobbing so hard I can't breathe.

The pit in my stomach has expanded to a void, and in it, anything and everything I could ever worry about writhes around, sending me into a spiral I've never been in before. I'm trying to run to get as far away from the house as possible so if they heard me, they wouldn't be able to find me. But my body is failing me, and the farther I get, the harder it is to continue on. Not only that, but these tears refuse to cease. Why am I crying so much? This is what I've wanted. This is what freedom feels like, isn't it? I'm out of that house, and I should feel great right about now.

Maybe I'm just not far enough.

I keep running.

My mind wanders to the darkness of the streets and the fear of what might lurk in the shadows. There aren't many streetlights here, and the ones that are around are so dim they only provide meager circles of flickering yellow that do nothing to light the way. The wind is cold against my face and blows my hair around, the golden strands swirling above my head. My tears almost feel frozen as they trail down my face in little silver rivers, perhaps looking like icicles in the wan moonlight. I sniffle against the runny nose that crying and cold have brought. For a split second, I try holding my breath to stop, but it only makes me sob harder.

But *why* am I crying? Is it because I'm stressed? That makes sense, considering I hastily threw this plan together in the heat of the moment. I try to repeat the plan to myself so I feel some semblance of reassurance as I trek into the dark.

First, I'm going to run in the direction of town. I remember seeing a bus stop when I went to the diner with Kai. I have loose change in my bag from ages ago which I'm sure will be enough for something. If it isn't, I will sneak on or beg them to let me hitch a ride or something. Whatever it is, I'm getting on that bus.

From there, I will go wherever the bus takes me. Preferably, I can get into the city somehow. There are tons of homeless shelters in the city; I even know of a few from when I used to live there. I'll get to the homeless shelter and live there for as long as I can and try to get money in any way. If I have to beg for it, I will. Once I have enough, I will get on another bus and go somewhere else. It doesn't matter where, just somewhere out of New York.

Even repeating this to myself does not help. My plan definitely isn't ideal, but I'm out, I remind myself. I'm away from the Kahales. *This is what I want.*

But it *still* isn't enough. I can't stop crying. I can hardly breathe. My head pounds from exertion and crying at the same time, and I start feeling dizzy and I know I have to stop.

Just for a second.

I walk to the sidewalk, moving out of the street, and lean against one of the streetlights. Even through my coat, I can feel the frozen metal trying to creep through my layers, but it is somehow grounding to feel the chill. Covering my face with my hands, I let myself cry loudly, holding onto the pole for the support my legs can't seem to give me right now. But it doesn't help when my intrusive thoughts infiltrate my brain with fervor, making me crumble to the ground in a little freezing heap.

I try to breathe, but it's too much. I can't do it. I can't get a breath in, can't get any air out. My chest stings, my muscles tighten, and my vision swims.

What's happening? What's happening?

I just have to keep going. It's this town. It isn't good for me here.

But those thoughts are beginning to seem less and less real the more I think of them. They don't seem right.

I look around helplessly, wanting to know where I am suddenly. I'm on a street I've never heard of before, and *of course,* I've never heard of it. I barely know this town, have barely given it a chance. So why would I know Mallard Lane? And why would I know where *town* is if I've only been there once?

And then, without precedent, I'm thinking, *I have to go back.* My breath catches at the mere prospect, the consequences of my actions seeping in. I *cannot* go back. I can't. They'll find out I ran away and they'll turn me in. Or they'll punish me, hurt me, make me feel worthless.

But... have the Kahales ever hurt me? Have they *ever* punished me or made me feel worthless?

Yes. Elise yelled at you.

Elise yelled at me, but I attacked her daughter first, didn't I? In a panic, I try recalling one instance where I felt unsafe in the Kahales' house. One time where I felt abused.

And as I rack my brain for anything, any semblance of fear or hurt, my blood runs cold in my veins. The world spins, stark darkness blurring around me. *Nothing comes to my mind.*

"What did I do?" I cry aloud, burying my face away once again. "What am I doing?"

My memories with the Kahales play in my mind. From the moment I stepped foot in their home, they've been nothing but kind to me. How have I been so blind to it? What's wrong with me?

What kind of person am I, to think this was some sort of manipulation technique, when in reality it was genuine kindness?

Elise has been trying to help me this whole time. Kai has been trying to get to know me and even let me come out with his friends. All I've done in return is verbally attack, criticize, and hurt them. And for what? Because they treated me with *respect*? Because they've never instilled fear in me for even a second?

What is wrong with you?

I take my phone out of my backpack and turn it on hastily. I *have* to go back. I don't know where I am, but maybe someone could come get me, and then—

I freeze as the missed calls flood in from every member of the Kahale family. There are tons. Then the messages come in, and I stand up as the alarm continues to circulate my body. I can't call them. What if they've called the police already? Or Jacob? If they have, I've been caught, and I can't get caught. That's the worst-case scenario, and if I tell them my location, getting caught will be my fate, which I cannot face.

I have no idea what to do. I'm such an idiot. I can't believe I did this to myself. Finally, I get to a place that's actually good for me, and I'm so self-destructive I run away from it, thinking they were literally trying to kill me with kindness. I could've had everything here. A family, siblings, a good school, friends. I even had something going with Emerson, and who knows what—

My train of thought is interrupted by a sudden realization. Immediately, I dig through my backpack, under all my clothes and notebooks, until I feel a crumpled piece of paper. Unfolding it, I take my first deep breath in a few moments and feel the cold touch my lungs.

There, in messy writing, is Emerson's phone number.

I dial her number without even thinking about it and eagerly wait as it rings. She picks up on the third ring.

"If this is a scam call, I don't own a car or a credit card, and I don't want to buy anything," Emerson says sassily.

Before I can stop myself, I laugh through my tears, covering my mouth to try and cover it up. I know she heard it, though.

"Uh... who is this?" she asks.

"It's Lavender. From school. You gave me your number in art—"

She gasps loudly. "Oh, my God. Why are you *calling* me right now? Not that I don't appreciate it, but it is a little weird since we've never even texted before."

"No, I know it's weird," I say honestly. I sniffle loudly and try to put coherent sentences together in my scrambled brain. "I know this is super weird, and it's okay if you want to hang up on me. But I did something really, really stupid, and I don't have anyone else's number in my phone so I don't have anyone else to call. I know, I'm practically a stranger, but I was wondering if you could do me a really big favor."

I hear her shifting around on her end. "You sound like you're crying. Lavender, are you okay? "

I shake my head sadly. "Honestly, no, I'm not okay. I made a really big mistake. I just need someone's help."

"Okay. Of course. What can I do?" she asks hurriedly, seeming confused but ready to do something.

"Can you come pick me up, please?" I feel like an idiot asking her this, but what other choice do I have? She's the only person who probably won't get me in trouble right now.

"Can you tell me what's going on?" Her voice turns steady and calm, coaxing, like she's talking to a fearful animal.

"I just—I made a mistake." I cover my face with my hands, shaking my head, in utter disbelief with myself. "I ran away from the Kahales, and I'm stranded on some street I've never heard of. I don't know how to get back, but I can't call the Kahales right now."

"Why can't you call them?" Her question is sad rather than condescending.

Defeated, I breathe, "I just can't. I'll be in trouble if I do. Do you think you can come?"

There is a minor hesitation, but she says, "Yes. Of course. Send me your location, and I'll be on my way."

In less than ten minutes, I see the first car I've seen all night pull up close to me. I can hardly see through the sheen of tears that coat my eyes, but I can very easily tell this car probably costs about as much as the Kahales' house—or maybe I just have a very skewed perception of money. Whatever the price may be, Emerson's car is luxury, and I might feel like a princess if I weren't at rock bottom. When the car comes to a full stop, I blindly open the door and sit down on a superbly heated, black leather seat, taking in the gentle blue lighting emitted from the dashboard.

Once I'm settled, I look at Emerson and see she looks extremely concerned. She asks, not unkindly, "Why did you call *me*?"

I sniff hard, trying to put off the crying for a minute so I can provide her with an answer in English rather than gibberish. "I had no one else to call. Seriously. I'm so sorry.

This is so weird, and I appreciate you coming so much. I know it's late, I'm sorry, I barely know anyone here, and I—"

"Whoa, okay, slow down," she interrupts, holding up her hands soothingly.

Instead of providing her with anything else useful, I blubber like a baby for another second, just to really reinforce I've completely screwed up my whole life.

"Okay, okay, it's okay," she says soothingly, leaning over the center console. "It's okay if you just wanna cry it out. We can talk later. I get it. I'm a Cancer, all I do is cry."

I laugh a little again through the tears. I'm amazed Emerson's already gotten me to laugh twice tonight despite my crisis.

Emerson smiles encouragingly. "Do you wanna breathe with me? Come on. I'll do it with you."

I nod slowly, unsure, but make eye contact with her when she gestures for me to look up. She breathes in deeply, and I try to follow, but my breathing is too irregular.

When I begin to panic over it, she smiles warmly again. "Hey, it's okay. We'll do it until you can do it. It's all right."

And we do. She patiently takes deep breaths with me until I can get a real good one, which helps me focus on breathing rather than crying. Then, I'm breathing normally with the occasional sniffle.

She lets us sit in a comfortable silence for a moment while I collect my thoughts. Then, she softly interrupts the moment by asking, "What happened?"

I look at her miserably. "I ran away."

"You mentioned," she says softly. "But why?"

Shaking my head, I wonder why myself. "I thought... I don't know what I thought. I made a mistake. I thought I didn't like it here, but I think I do. And I might... want to stay. But it doesn't matter what I want. I can't stay anymore."

Emerson doesn't understand. "Why can't you, though? I can take you back to the Kahales and you could explain what happened."

"No," I insist, voice breaking. "I'm sure they've called my social worker by now. Or the police. If I'm caught, I can't stay."

"What? What kind of rule is that?"

I shrug, running a hand through my tangled hair.

"Well, why don't I call Kai first? We can see what's going on, and I'll make him swear not to tell if he says they already called the police or whoever."

I look at her hesitantly. Shutting my eyes, I admit, "I'm too scared."

Her face softens, all joking and lightheartedness draining from her tone. "It'll be okay. I swear to you, it will be okay. Whatever happens, I'll be here."

After a second of considering, I finally nod, giving Emerson permission to call Kai.

They have a brief conversation themselves before getting me involved, but they quickly jump out of the small talk.

"Look, Kai, I have to tell you something, but you can't get upset," Emerson begins. Even though I can't hear what Kai's saying, I can tell from Emerson's grimace it might not be good. "I know. I know you're stressed right now. Lavender is with me, though, Kai."

There is a long pause where I can assume Kai is panicking or asking a bunch of questions. Emerson rolls her eyes and looks at me with annoyance written in her soft features.

"Sounds like you're getting real upset, real fast," Emerson points out. "Can you just let me explain, please?"

Emerson goes on to explain how I contacted her, and I sit with my knees pulled up to my chin in the passenger seat, trying to slow the thoughts racing through my head.

Emerson must think this is so weird, and I know it really isn't my business what Emerson thinks of me, but it matters for some reason.

"Yes, she's perfectly safe, I promise," Emerson reassures him, her hand tapping mindlessly against her steering wheel to an invisible beat. "I wouldn't lie to you about something like this. She's right here with me. She's obviously upset but she is physically perfect. More than perfect."

She gives me a sideways glance that makes my stomach do flips, and I bury my face so I don't have to face it.

"Will you guys make sure they know it was a false alarm, though?" she asks.

I feel my heart race uncomfortably quick at that. Who did the Kahales contact? The police? Jacob? *Both*?

"Oh, you didn't call the police." I lift my eyes slightly to see Emerson giving me a reassuring look. "Okay, so just make sure that guy knows it's a false alarm. Say she was sneaking out to see me or something." There's a pause, and Emerson's face fills with disgust. "Well, how am I supposed to know how this works? Just tell him to back off!"

Maybe I'd laugh if this situation wasn't what it is, but right now, I don't even crack a smile.

"No, no, you don't need to come get her. She's coming home with me," Emerson says casually.

"Wait, what?" I ask confusedly, but she just waves me off.

"Maybe it's better for her to have a night away, Kai." She looks at me, hesitates, then continues. "She ran away for a reason. She'll be safe with me. I'll bring her home tomorrow morning."

It takes a little bit of convincing, but after Elise supposedly gets on the phone to confirm this, I am given permission to stay with Emerson for the night. As soon as she hangs up the phone, she puts her hand on my shoulder and tells me everything is going to be okay, and for a moment, it truly doesn't feel real. I'd expected the worst, and it didn't happen for once. Maybe I can actually go on living with the Kahales as if none of this happened, but this time I won't mess it up. Maybe I can even enjoy it this time around.

"Thank you," I say genuinely. "This is a lot, I know, and I'm really grateful you—"

"Don't mention it." She offers me a small smile. "We all have our stuff, Lavender. I'm happy to help."

I smile in return and watch as she switches the car's gearshift into drive. And I'm on my way to Emerson's house, a swarm of pesky butterflies flitting around in my stomach at every turn.

CHAPTER TEN

The car ride with Emerson is weirdly relaxing. Her car smells like expensive perfume and nighttime, and the music that plays from the car speakers is gentle. She looks over at me several times on the way, as if making sure I'm still there, but I don't say anything. I'm a little embarrassed about the entire situation, and though Emerson has made me feel perfectly comfortable, I can't shake that feeling.

Emerson turns right onto a brightly lit street with huge houses. I realize quickly the street also has underground powerlines. Looking at the homes, I try to remember if the Kahales' house actually looks like this, if I've been oblivious to it the entire time. But the sizes and grandeur of these houses far surpass the Kahales, no matter how cozy and expensive their house is. These houses must be a billion dollars. There are several driveways with more than four cars in them. At least three have circular driveways, fountains, and terrifying statues that would look better outside of a church.

I'm wondering when we're going to turn off this street to get to Emerson's when she begins pulling up to a house on the left.

We drive up to easily the most beautiful one on the block, and I'm saying that without even seeing it in the daylight. It is lit in such a way it seems intimidating and massive. Christmas lights outline the roof and lines of the house, but they're so perfect and expensive-looking, it almost takes all the fun out of having Christmas lights at all.

My jaw to the floor, I try to form a coherent thought so I can fill the suddenly awkward silence. "I—"

Emerson interrupts me before I can say anything, though. "I know, it's crazy I live here because I'm so humble and down to earth, but yes, my parents are filthy rich, emphasis on the *filthy* part. I hate it but can't do much about it, so when the shock wears off, it's probably best if we don't bring it up again. Okay?"

I nod, amusement swimming in my eyes as I look at Emerson. She's ashamed of where she lives which helps me understand she might really be as humble as she says, even though she meant it as a complete joke.

The two of us get out of Emerson's car, which I now realize is a BMW. I almost choke on my spit when I realize I've just sobbed my eyes out in a BMW with tinted windows, but I remember Emerson's embarrassment and swallow hard, trying to ignore it.

I feel like I'm walking up to a fortress as I navigate the steep, grand staircase. I felt something similar to the day I moved in with the Kahales, but this is something else entirely. I am a literal piece of trash in comparison to everything on the premises. Even their trash can is clean and polished, so what does that make me?

But, I remind myself, Emerson isn't wearing a ballgown or a Gucci belt. She's wearing sweatpants and a baggy sweatshirt. Both of which look beautiful on her, but that's not the point.

The point is I shouldn't feel ashamed of myself. I shouldn't, but that doesn't make the feeling go away.

"Please don't look like that," Emerson says, and I realize she's been studying me closely.

"Like what?" I ask cluelessly.

She laughs lightly. "Like you're about to cry again. Whatever you're thinking, I want you to know, this whole house is my parents' and not mine. I know I live here, but that doesn't mean I have the same brain as they do. But, man, they'd love that, wouldn't they?"

I don't really know what she's talking about, but I nod slowly and follow her up the million steps to the double mahogany front doors. They even have some silver and scary-looking knockers on them, and I wonder if anybody actually uses them. I feel tiny and unimportant walking into the huge entryway behind Emerson.

I'm immediately immersed in cold, white lights that somehow remind me of the fluorescent ones at most schools. Even though the glow comes from a chandelier bigger than Emerson's car, it feels clinical and detached, not like the warmth I feel in the Kahales' home. Aside from this, every piece of furniture appears to never have been used. Each cushion and pillow looks like stone, like it's on display at a museum for viewing only. And all of this could be okay, *is* okay if that's what Emerson's family likes, until I really take in the decor. The zebra skin rug, the stuffed deer on display in the living room. Something about it made me feel chilled to the bone, then angry, because I know rich people feel entitled enough to put these things on display, no matter how morally wrong it is.

Before I can stop myself, I exclaim, "Oh, you've *got* to be kidding me."

Emerson bursts into laughter. "What'd you see first? The zebra skin rug, the white piano, or the crystal chandelier? Because I have the same reaction whenever I walk in here, too."

"I just—I mean, I know you don't like bringing it up, I—like, how do you even... how could one person be so *rich*?"

Emerson looks at me point-blank. "The only way to get this type of money is, one, be a dick. And two, partake in the most boring careers known to man. Bonus points if you have zero hobbies other than turning your nose up."

I follow Emerson further into the house, past the insanely large staircase into a bright hallway, taking in the sleek home. "How can you even think that if you live here?"

"I know. I'm a hypocrite. I guess I haven't figured out the best way to get out of here yet. Maybe after college. Or maybe I should just take off after high school. But I really do want a college education, and from there, we'll see about cutting my parents off from my lovely company."

"Where are they? Do you have a second house in the back that belongs to them or something?"

Emerson giggles. "Unfortunately, no, this is all I have to offer you right now. But they're away, on business. They spend half their time here and half their time in our penthouse in the city." She scrunches her nose up. "I hate them. I really do."

I shake my head. "You don't really mean that, right? I mean, they're your parents."

As we walk into the kitchen, filled with stainless steel appliances and white, marble countertops, Emerson stops and turns to look at me. There's an apologetic look on her face. "I'm sorry. I know that sounds insensitive."

"No, I mean, I don't really care. I guess it's just hard for me to understand how you could hate your parents if they're, well... there."

Emerson gestures around, smiling dryly. "Well, are they? Here?"

I cross my arms, realizing her point. I nod slowly and follow her to the kitchen island. Emerson goes about busying herself in cupboards and cabinets, and I stand there awkwardly watching, not really sure what she's doing or what I should be doing.

"Would you like a snack?" she asks. "I know it's late, but midnight snacks happen to be my favorite."

My initial reaction is to say no, but I have a thought I've never had before. What would be the harm in sharing a midnight snack with Emerson? I feel the regular hesitation, wondering if it's worth it to allow myself to get close to someone else, but now I'm wondering if maybe that might be all right. Scary, but all right, because even if I have to end up leaving here, at least I'll have one positive memory for the books. Right?

So I shrug. "Yeah, sure. Why not?"

Emerson looks satisfied at that, and when she asks what I want, I tell her I'm not picky. She ends up making popcorn on the stovetop, which I've never done before. She also makes some organic macaroni and cheese, which I think is funny.

"How come they make instant food for rich people? Can't you just hire chefs for that?" I ask sarcastically, watching as she strains the pasta.

"Hey! Just because it's organic doesn't mean it's for rich people," she replies with a laugh. "And we definitely don't have a chef. I fend for myself, and organic mac n' cheese is what I like to eat."

"Got it." I find these little details endearing. I've always been fascinated how people who aren't me live their lives, even if the things they do are commonplace.

When both the popcorn and mac n' cheese are done, Emerson serves me, and we sit side by side at the island on black leather stools. Everything is really good, and I wonder if she actually does buy more expensive food just because she can. It's a simple concept, but it's hard for me to understand because I've never really had money.

"So," Emerson says when we're halfway through our food. "Luke told me about today."

For a second I'm confused, forgetting this day had other components besides the monumental event that happened toward the end. But my memory kicks in. "Oh. I... it was a complete misunderstanding, and I—"

"Were you gonna do it, Lavender? Were you gonna kill yourself tonight?" she asks bluntly, looking in my eyes intensely.

I put my spoon down, feeling my face pale under the fluorescent kitchen lights. "No. I wasn't. I said I wasn't coming back because I planned on running away or getting kicked out or something. I'd never do that to myself."

"Do you promise?" Her eyes hold a heaviness I haven't seen from her before. There isn't a hint of her little smirk or any amusement in her brown eyes. It makes me feel like I owe her my safety, strangely enough.

I find it weird she asks me to, but I promise her anyway. Silence fills the space between us. We both stare at our food. With the weight of where our conversation has gone, I no longer feel the lightheartedness that was present before. I don't feel like joking or making sarcastic comments. I don't think Emerson does either, and the way she stares down at the table, looking pale and hesitant, makes me wonder if I've done something wrong.

The air weighs heavier when Emerson says, "I've thought about it. About... doing that before."

“What?” I breathe, feeling the air sucked out of my lungs. Her words strike me deep in my chest.

Emerson swallows hard. Her eyes are guarded but sad. “I don’t think that way anymore. I swear, I don’t. But I was really lonely in middle school. It was before I met Luke and made friends, and my parents were never around. I thought they hated me. And they never saw me, anyway, never even called me to check-in. So I just thought…” She sighs and brushes hair from her forehead. “I don’t know what I thought. But that time in my life is over now.”

“I’m sorry you went through that. That’s no way for parents to treat their child. No one deserves that,” I say, hoping I sound as genuine as I feel. A piece of my heart hurts for her, but also yearns for her. Something about the loneliness she describes speaks to me so loudly I can’t ignore it.

Suddenly, Emerson begins to laugh. It’s quiet at first, but she’s laughing so hard she’s gripping the table. For a moment I think the whole story she told me was fake, and I prematurely feel anger rushing through me, but she looks at me and I forget the anger.

“I can’t believe you’re apologizing to me, Lavender. You went through so much tonight. *I’m* sorry, I had no right to tell you that. I just... I felt like I—”

“I know,” I say. “I know what you mean. There’s no reason to be sorry.”

“Okay.” She smiles. “Thanks.”

Another silence fills the air, but silences around Emerson are comfortable. I don’t feel awkward or like I need to say anything. It feels nice to sit in silence with her and talk about nothing, because somehow, words aren’t needed all the time. In some crazy way, maybe Emerson understands some things about my life, and maybe I understand some things about hers, too.

Emerson's face lights up as I'm looking at her out of the corner of my eye, and I pick my head up, wondering what thoughts are going through her head.

"Hey, you wanna do something really fun?" she asks.

I look at her skeptically. "Okay, no offense, but what's your definition of 'fun?'"

She looks offended but in a comical way. As she stands, she says, "Nothing weird. I promise. Now get up and help me with something."

I do as she says and follow her down a hallway to a series of rooms. We walk into one with glass doors that looks like a den. It has a huge couch, a TV, and a computer desk with an office chair to match.

Emerson walks to a bin filled to the top with blankets and grabs a stack. She hands the stack to me, then grabs a few more. I follow her back into the living room, and she leads me to the back door.

"We're going outside?" I ask, thinking of the chill out there. As much as I love the cold, I don't know how much I want to bathe in it right now.

"Just trust me," she says.

She opens the door, and a blast of cold air hits me right in the face. I shiver, and Emerson laughs at me, but I can see she's shaking too.

The back door opens out to a finished, wooden deck that is much too large. I mean, who needs this much deck space?

Emerson tells me to drop the blankets once we reach a particular spot she chooses, and after I do, she follows my lead. She tells me to wait for her to come back out, so I sit on the freezing cold deck and wait for her to come back.

After a good few minutes pass, I start to feel like an idiot. Did she leave me here or something? Was her plan to humiliate me somehow all long?

After another few, I expect to see Luke coming out of the bushes with a camera, but that doesn't happen. Instead, Emerson comes outside with two huge, steaming mugs, and I pray to whoever's listening it's hot chocolate and not coffee.

She hands me one and says, "I hope you like marshmallows, because I put a thick layer on there for you."

I laugh and thank her, then take a deep sip out of the mug. The flavor is rich and dark, warming my throat and stomach so wonderfully in the chill. When I set it down, I realize in the porch lighting she's given me a lavender cup. I smile to myself, but I don't say anything.

"So what are we doing out here?" I ask nonchalantly.

Emerson doesn't reply, though. She walks to a corner of the deck and flips a switch. As soon as she does, I feel heat coming toward me from that corner. She does the same thing a few more times at the edges of the deck until she's turned on a bunch of heaters and the space is already warmer.

"One more thing," she says absentmindedly, disappearing into the house.

While she's gone, the porch lights go out, and I'm submerged in the pitch black of nighttime.

Emerson appears again and helps me fix up the blankets. Once we're both sitting down on the deck, I look at her expectantly.

"I repeat, what are we doing?"

Emerson looks excited and giddy. She points upward. "Look up."

I do, and I'm struck by a beauty I've never taken a smidge of time to appreciate.

"The stars," Emerson says quietly. "We're stargazing."

I laugh as I stare up, my warm breath showing in the air. Looking between Emerson and the sky, I'm in utter bewilderment at the fact she had this idea, she went through with it, and I'm here right now.

"Lay with me?" she asks, and I lay.

Then we're in silence again, looking at the stars, thinking. I have no clue what Emerson's thinking, but all I'm doing is wondering what's on her mind. It isn't a productive thought sequence, but I find myself continuously asking myself, *What do you think she's thinking about now? What about now?* That is, until I look at her, and she is lost in the stars above.

Her expression, even from the side, is one of longing and passion, but I don't know how to explain it other than that. It's almost like she's looking for something up there. It's poetic, really, and surreal. To see her like that, to be where I am after the day I've had.

And then I'm thinking about the day I've had. I'm thinking about how absolutely devastated the Kahales probably were. I don't know how they found out I was gone, but I can imagine it must have been stressful for everyone. Maybe they panicked. Maybe they were worried about me and missing me. Maybe Leia was crying. My heart drops at the thought. *Leia.* What have I done to her?

Out of nowhere, Emerson asks, "Lavender, do you actually like girls, or was I way off?"

I laugh quietly as my thoughts dissipate, and I'm brought back to the moment. I turn my head to the left, stare at Emerson's shadowed face. The lines of her face are smooth, I notice. "Yes, I like girls. And boys, too. Though I'm not proud of that last part."

This time, Emerson laughs, but the chuckles rack her body until her eyes are shutting and her mouth opening in a way that is contagious. A smile breaks my lips apart as well and I watch her laugh and laugh, just like at the table not too long ago.

"I remember when I thought I liked boys, too," Emerson says. "It was *horrible*. And when I finally figured it out, that it was just girls, it was worse with boys somehow. They always think they can change me."

"I understand," I say. "I understand how frustrating it is when people want to change you."

"Do you?"

I nod, looking back up at the sky above. A breeze ruffles my hair, blowing it in front of my face, and before I can brush it away, Emerson is sitting up and doing it for me. My stomach turns, face turning bright red, and I look away.

"I'm sorry," Emerson says quietly. "Did that make you uncomfortable?"

I shake my head but don't look at her yet. "I don't really like being touched... but it wasn't so bad that time."

Emerson nods with a small smile. She doesn't lay back down, and I think of sitting up as well, but I'm just too content here. Plus, it's kind of nice, the way she's looking at me like *I'm* the stars instead now. Her face still reads like a poem, and I wonder what mine looks like.

"Who tried to change you?" Emerson asks, her voice still soft.

The question draws me away from Emerson's shining eyes, right back down to earth, where I'm not the stars, but a ratty foster kid in front of a rich girl living a life of luxury.

"Everyone tries to change me," I state quietly. "I've been called a 'problem child' since my first panic attack at age six. I was on my third home in a matter of months, and I couldn't handle being tossed around so much. I freaked out when leaving one. I couldn't breathe, could barely see anything. It manifested itself as anger, which, you know... became my reputation or whatever."

Emerson shakes her head gently. "But you were only six."

"I know." I shrug, looking past her so I don't begin to cry again tonight. "From there it was easier to be angry than to let myself feel anything else. I didn't want to feel anything else. I barely had room inside me, anyway, because of how angry I was. I still am angry."

After a moment of silence, Emerson says, "I'd be angry too. I would've run away a long time ago."

I laugh humorlessly. "Not if you were me. Not if you had so much to lose."

"What do you mean?"

"I mean I made the coward's move today without thinking about it. I mean I put myself in jeopardy because of my stupid *anger.* All it does is consume me. I shouldn't have run away. It was the wrong decision. Other kids who do that aren't as lucky as I was tonight."

Emerson looks at me fiercely. "What do they do, lock you in a dungeon? Feed you to dragons?"

"You're not way off." I sigh. "I most likely would've gone to juvie if I'd been caught."

This sends her speechless, and she looks away. I'm worried I've scared her, and for some reason, I genuinely hope I haven't.

I sit up slowly, feel the blankets fall off my shoulders softly. "I didn't get caught, though, Emerson. I'm still here."

She looks at me. In her eyes is something I can't identify. *Is* it fear? Has what I said made her fearful, upset in some way?

"You won't always be, though, will you?"

The question brings me up short. Up until today, I would've told her I'd be gone in a matter of days, but now

I don't even know. Of course, every foster child dreams of finding a place they can stay and call home. For me, it would be great if it were the Kahales, but who knows what will happen when I get back tomorrow? If I get through that, what could happen in two months? Six months? Longer? There's simply no way to know right now.

But, I realize, Emerson does look worried. Like if I told her I was leaving, she'd be devastated. I could be way off, but something in my gut tells me to reassure her, to cast her worries aside.

"I will be," I say. It feels like a lie even though I don't know for sure it is. "I'm not going anywhere, Emerson."

When I look back up at the stars to see what they have to say about it, a snowflake touches my cheek. I smile.

CHAPTER ELEVEN

"Hey," the soft voice says, and I lean into its embrace. Here, it is warm and everything is gentle against me. I am not wholly me, but I am not wholly something else, either. I am safely tucked into this pocket between me and not me, awake and asleep, conscious and unconscious. And here, the warm light pours beyond my closed eyes and paints everything golden. And here, I feel nothing but this warmth.

"Lavender, you gotta get up," the voice says, with an increasing sense of urgency.

As I open my eyes to meet this voice, I am struck by a bright light that hurts my eyes, and as I take in a deep breath, I smell something unfamiliar but cozy. Cinnamon, oranges, the clean smell of detergent. Distantly, expensive perfume that definitely has jasmine in it.

"Are you awake or just pretending again?" Emerson asks, laughter lacing her words.

I pick my head up and look around. At first, my surroundings are unfamiliar, but my memory comes back.

After stargazing for the better part of the entire night, Emerson and I came up to her bedroom to sleep. She gave me her sweatshirt because she said mine wasn't keeping me warm enough—but she was really just flirting with me—and we both fell asleep shortly after. I fell asleep in a huge pile of blankets on the floor, and she fell asleep in her king-sized bed, which she asked me multiple times if I wanted to share, but I declined every time. I don't know how I feel about sharing a bed with anyone just yet.

"What?" I ask groggily. "What time is it?"

"It's noon," Emerson says calmly. She comes and sits on the floor in front of me.

She looks perfect, as always. Her hair is back in two French braids, both done neatly. Her hair is still wet from a shower from the looks of it, but a few stubborn pieces hair frame her face in gentle but messy waves. She wears pale pink sweatpants and a long-sleeved white shirt that looks really soft.

"Noon?" I repeat frantically, my energy spiking. "Why didn't you wake me for school hours ago?"

Emerson shrugs, looking content with her decision. "I spoke to Kai early this morning, and he said his mom stayed home from work to be home for you anyway. I told him you were up late last night and all of us mutually decided to let you sleep in. Is that okay?"

I nod as I sit up, though it feels strange people have been discussing me. Perhaps this is the feeling of being cared for, something I am unfamiliar with.

My back aches from laying on the floor, and I groan while stretching it out. Emerson watches me carefully.

"That's fine. Thanks," I say, wondering what this look is about.

"Yeah, no problem." But she keeps looking at me curiously.

In return, I offer her a quizzical glance, wondering if I've done something wrong. "What is it?"

"You're funny when you're sleeping."

I grow even more confused. Rubbing my eyes, I wonder if I'm mishearing because I'm so tired. "Excuse me?"

Emerson laughs. "I thought you woke up, like, three times in the night, but it was like you were just pretending. You looked around and I asked if you were okay, but every time you just gave me a rude look and went back to sleep."

I laugh despite myself. "Are you joking?"

"Not at all."

I've never heard that before, but I guess I've never been in the position where someone would tell me that.

In the back of my mind, I can't help but think about how intimate a detail like that is to know about someone. I'm probably overthinking it, but I've never had a sleepover with someone before. Is it supposed to feel this intimate?

"I never knew I did that," I say, shrugging. "Thanks for the info, though."

"Oh, of course." She leans back on her palms and does not stop looking at me. Maybe it's just a mannerism of hers—direct and unending eye contact—but it's starting to make me feel a little self-conscious. I'm not used to someone staring at me with such forwardness. Before I can say anything about it, she asks, "Do you want breakfast?"

I nod eagerly. "Yeah, definitely."

Surprisingly, Emerson isn't a bad cook. She makes me eggs and breakfast potatoes, sets out some fresh fruit, and even though everything is simple, it's really good and makes me feel happy. She eats a bit with me but tells me she ate more before, so it's pretty much just my appetite and me working through the food.

While eating, I take a look at my phone. I see the same amount of texts and calls as last night, with a few added texts from Elise and Kai reiterating what Emerson told me about today. Other than looking at these messages, I do not look at anything else. I hardly want to remember last night at all, even though the biggest mistake of my life ended with probably the best night of my life. Confusing, yes, but so many other things, too. Exciting, for one thing. And, I don't know... maybe I might have a crush on Emerson. Maybe.

What I do know is I have very little time to think about it. Last night was a good distraction for me, but it's time to get back to my real life, where I don't get to sleep in mansions and spend my nights staring at the stars.

When I'm finished eating, I politely ask Emerson to take me back to the Kahales. She agrees and helps me gather my things. When I try to take off her sweatshirt, she tells me to give it to her tomorrow since it'll be cold outside now, anyway. She ignores me when I tell her I have my own sweatshirt.

We drive home in the same comfortable silence that's followed us around since last night. Only the car's heating fills the space this morning, and I look out my window contentedly, watching the houses and trees go by.

Finally, Emerson pulls into the Kahales' driveway. It feels weird to get out. I almost don't want to. I know when I do, this will end, and that in itself feels like a nightmare. This moment between Emerson and I will likely not change anything in our regular lives, which also scares me. The feelings I felt with Emerson last night were so new and foreign and, yes, terrifying, but also so welcome and warm. I want to feel like that again. But something tells me getting out of this car will mean I never will.

"So... I guess I'll see you at school tomorrow, then," I say softly.

When I look over at Emerson, her expression is disappointed, maybe even apologetic. She might feel the same way

I do, which makes me feel slightly better. Maybe if she feels it, too, we can prevent it from changing. I try to convince myself of this, but it's too hard to believe.

"Yeah. I guess you will," she replies with a detached aloofness that is so unlike her. You don't need to know Emerson for more than a day to know she's good at expressing herself, and I can't help but feel unsettled at the change. Could she be upset she won't be seeing me like this again? Does she want me to stay? Or is she somehow sick of me and just wanting me to get out of the car?

I nod once and give her a stiff smile that feels awkward and weird. Without saying anything else, I grab my backpack and get out. I look back to wave once, then head into the house to deal with my unresolved issues from last night.

Walking into the brightly-lit foyer, I'm struck with the familiar scent of the Kahale household: something like cinnamon and citrus. The room is brightly lit with sunlight, the windows casting square-shaped shadows against the wood floor.

As soon as I close the door, Elise walks quickly toward me, and I'm immediately shoved back by the force of her hug. She wraps her arms around me as tight as possible and squeezes the life out of me, nearly sweeping me off my feet. I return the hug for once, not feeling uncomfortable but feeling safe. Safe and happy and okay. My throat aches, threatening tears, but I swallow hard to make it go away.

After a few long seconds, Elise pulls away and looks at me. Her face is controlled, but her eyes hold the motherly concern I wrote off as fake this whole time.

"Let's go sit in the living room," she says. I nod and follow her.

We settle on the couch and look at each other, and my stomach is turning, but it's different than anxiety or the feeling I get with Emerson. I suppose I could say it's nervous-excitement, but that isn't right either. The only way I can describe it is I'm horrified to hear all about Elise's disappointment in me, but I'm looking forward to showing her I can do better, I *want* to do better. So many new feelings lately, and it's becoming harder and harder to place them.

"Are you okay?" she asks, as if she's been waiting to ask this for hours.

I laugh with relief, happy we're easing into this. I know Elise probably wouldn't be the type to scream and yell, but it's still a relieving confirmation. "Yes. I'm perfectly okay."

She lets out a sigh, laughing a bit herself, then becomes serious once more. "Is there anything you want to tell me?"

I look away, but I have to say this. "Yes to that, too. I want to apologize first. I treated all of you awfully without even realizing why I was doing what I was doing, but I know now and I'm going to try my best. I'm not excusing what I've done, but I'm used to having to protect myself. I've never been somewhere I *didn't* have to protect myself. I don't know how to be cared for. And for that, I really am sorry. I am going to try to do better.

"I also acknowledge I think I need help to truly do better. You mentioned counseling, which I think is a really great idea. I thought it was terrifying when you first brought it up, but I thought about Leia and how much it would benefit her to be in counseling, and I realized it isn't as scary as I made it out to be. And I think Leia and I should go together. Different therapists, obviously, but we could go at the same time, or whatever. Maybe that would make her less nervous about it."

Elise looks at me with an expression I don't think I've ever seen before. It takes me a minute to place the look, but maybe Elise is actually proud of me right now. Maybe I've done well. Maybe this is the right choice, and it will only go up from here.

"Lavender, I think that's a really great idea," she says, and it sounds like she's holding back from jumping with joy. "I will set that up for the both of you as soon as I can."

I let out a sigh of relief myself, and it feels cleansing. Like I've gotten something off my chest, which I suppose I have. But it's more than that. No one's ever looked at me with pride. It makes me feel light and joyful inside, almost giddy. I could definitely get used to this feeling.

"I'm really proud of you for coming to these conclusions on your own and for making decisions for yourself that will benefit you." Hearing she's proud of me makes my entire body swell with warmth, and I try my best to hide my smile that so badly wants to break through, because I know I'm still in trouble here. Elise knows it too, and despite the happiness in her expression, she becomes a bit more serious as she continues. "I also want to remind you my family treats people with respect, and I expect you to do the same here. Okay? That's all I want."

I nod firmly. "Of course. I will do that."

She looks hesitant, but after a beat of silence asks, "What happened, Lavender? Why did you feel like you had to run away?"

I look down at my lap and squeeze my hands together, feeling the pressure of it ground me in this moment, because I know she deserves an explanation, and I know it's important I provide her with one. It's the least I can do.

"I don't know, Elise," I say on a breath out. "I guess I convinced myself I wasn't safe here. But that isn't true, and I know that now. I felt trapped, like this isn't the healthiest environment I've ever been in." I sigh, running a hand through my knotted hair.

Meeting Elise's eyes, I take note of the concerned furrow in her brow. Just another reminder of how genuine she is. She cares. She's concerned, and I appreciate it. Maybe it's selfish, but I want people to be concerned for me. I never gave into that want before right now, but what's the use in pretending it doesn't exist? What's the use in denying my own thoughts and emotions for the life I shouldn't have to live? I should be able to feel cared for. I deserve concern.

"I thought I wanted to go back to the way things were, before I came here," I continue slowly. "I'm just not used to your family yet. I'm used to something... different. But I'm going to work harder on myself, on the way I am. I know I have a long way to go."

She nods. Slowly, Elise reaches her hand up and I watch as it touches my shoulder. Though my skin tingles because of this contact I'm not used to, I don't pull away. I don't shove her off me.

"You do have a long way to go, and I expect you to put the work in. I know you can," Elise says, holding the eye contact. "But we're here for you. Talk to us, to me. You can't do something like that again. It isn't safe for you, you know? There's little we can do if CPS gets involved."

I nod knowingly, taking a deep breath. "I know. And I'm sorry. I really am. I'm going to put the work in."

She nods back, looking at me sadly, but there's a smile in there, too. That's just how Elise is, I'm beginning to learn. She has sympathy and doesn't want to be that controlling person in my life I've gotten so used to. It's why her children are so kind. It's why I'm willing to be better.

"Let's start with a few responsibilities around the house," Elise suggests.

"You mean as a punishment?" I ask, biting the inside of my cheek. I know I deserve punishment, but it worries me I'll start having unhelpful thoughts again if the Kahales really put me to work.

"Don't think of it as a punishment." Elise considers her next words. "It's just a way for you to show us you're willing to do better, to work on it, like we just talked about. How about you wash the dishes after dinner a few times a week? You can alternate with Kai and Leia."

"Oh," I breathe out. "You just want me to wash the dishes?"

"What, did you think I'd make you wash the roof?" Elise laughs, and I respond with a hesitant grin. She grows serious when she sees my face. "Has someone actually made you wash their roof?"

I'm beginning to say no, no one ever has before, but she interrupts me, saying, "Actually, don't tell me. I don't want to know. It would probably break my heart."

I smile at the way she rests her hand over her heart, like she can feel it shattering at the mere image of me scrubbing a roof with my bare hands.

"Now, Kai told me you were up all night, so why don't you get some rest?" The sad look is wiped from her face as she straightens. "We'll talk more later when everyone else gets home, all right?"

I agree and accept a second hug when she offers it simply because I want Elise to understand I want to be all in here. I might not be going around hugging strangers anytime soon, but I need to allow myself to loosen up a little bit if I'm comfortable with it. And, as it turns out, it isn't so bad.

Afterward, I make my way upstairs with my backpack and look around at the room I actually thought I'd never see again. I'm glad I'm back. There's nowhere else I'd rather be.

I get into bed in what I'm wearing, feeling oddly attached to the pink, cropped sweatshirt Emerson let me take. It's completely plain and oversized, worn at the cuffs like she's had it for years. And even though I don't feel that tired, I fall asleep quickly, drifting once again into unconsciousness.

I wake to arms thrown around me, and for a moment, I go into panic mode, until I realize the person is squealing like a little girl, and I realize it *is* a little girl.

"Leia!" I say excitedly, still bleary-eyed but happy to see her.

"You came back," she says, obvious relief written on her face. "I'm really glad you came back."

We hug tightly, and I'm amazed by the way I don't feel too uncomfortable by this. Perhaps it's just because I'm so relieved to be here, but I don't mind it today.

Just then, Kai makes his way in. He runs and jumps on my bed extremely noisily. Something makes a loud banging noise and Leia and I look at Kai in shock. We hear Elise yell from downstairs, "What'd you break, Kai!" but Kai just yells back jumbled words that don't make sense to throw his mom off.

"Hey," I say with a smile.

"Hey back!" he says, bumping my shoulder with his.

"I'm sorry for being an asshat," I say in a serious tone.

He gives me an equally serious tone when he says, "I completely forgive you for being an asshat."

There's something between Kai and I that goes past my relationship with anyone else here—when I really think about it, Kai might be the only person I've *really* spoken to so far since I refused to let anyone else in and I had to see Kai for school. It makes me embarrassed for the millionth time just because of the ways I've repressed any sort of connection with him whatsoever. Sending him to the principal's office, making fun of his relationship with his mom. In general, my behavior has not been a positive experience for anyone, but I feel like Kai got caught in the crossfire more than anyone else.

It means a lot to me he's able to joke with me like he's able to joke with Leia.

"Thanks," I say. "Really, I appreciate it."

Leia interrupts the sincere moment, clearly finished with apologies and tearful reunions. Giggling, she says, "Kai, *you're* the asshat."

Kai facepalms, looking disappointed. "You can't say asshat!"

But she just laughs and shoves her brother into the wall, getting him involved in some typical sibling banter that has always made me feel a little weird, but now it just makes me feel... content. It makes me feel good.

When the banter stops, Leia looks at me and asks, "Lavender, will you watch a movie with us tonight?"

It takes no thought to decide. For the first time, I say yes.

CHAPTER TWELVE

It's harder than I thought to get used to a life filled with respect and calmness. It's like I was so focused on hating my life and self I built up a barrier that kept out anything positive. And now I have this positivity forcing its way through the barrier, it's terrifying, because what if it's fake? What if I'm being mocked? What if I get hurt? What if I have to leave here?

Not only that, but it occurs to me maybe I've always done this. Maybe I haven't ever given anyone the slightest chance to get to know me, to care about me, out of fear and self-preservation.

The effort to reteach my brain the proper way to respond to people, to live life, to think, has proven to be nearly impossible because I feel so alone in it. Sure, the Kahales are here, but could they ever really understand where I'm coming from? Probably not. The years of trauma instilled in me from failed placement after failed placement have hardwired my brain to work differently. It isn't anyone's fault they could never understand, but it does mean I might truly be alone in fixing this.

It hasn't been as instantaneous as I can tell the Kahales were hoping. But I can't help but be hesitant. I can't help I still need distance. I can't help I find myself questioning simple things and spiraling into negative thought patterns.

What matters, however, is I actively try to combat those negative thoughts now because of how far from the truth they have steered me. My own intuition failed me at a moment where that type of failure could've placed me in juvie.

It's particularly difficult for me to understand unsolicited niceness from the Kahales, who will sometimes mention moments when they thought of me throughout the day or even ask me to choose dinner for the night. On Wednesday, Elise actually comes home with a throw blanket that reminds her of me, which sends me into a spiral.

Do I owe her something? Does she expect me to pay for it? Do I have to give her something in return? Why did she do this? Am I allowed to have it, to actually use it?

The blanket was embroidered with lavender all over it, and it made my heart so warm and I wanted to use it so badly I asked Elise, quite boldly, why she got it for me, why she gave it to me.

"I wanted you to have something new!" she said with a smile on her face. "I know it's cheesy it has lavender on it, but I thought it was beautiful. If you don't like it, I can take it back."

"No, no," I said frantically. "I love it. It *is* beautiful. Thank you."

After this interaction, I held the blanket to my chest, feeling the softness against my skin. I ran upstairs to my room to drape it on my bed, looked at it proudly. *My* blanket. Something brand new, just for me. The feeling it gave me was profound, thrilling.

It has begun to occur to me Elise might show her love by spending money. I'm sure it has nothing to do with money, though it is what strikes me about this attribute of her. Buying this blanket for me, bringing home Kai's favorite candies, buying Leia a book about outer space because she mentioned she wanted to learn about it. It's Elise's way of loving, and she doesn't expect anything in return. A thank-you is, of course, always nice, but she does it to see the widening of Leia's eyes, to feel the gratitude in Kai's hug.

It brings tears to my eyes, knowing I might actually be wanted here.

I think this through as I eat dinner on Thursday night. I sit next to Leia, who's having an intense conversation with her brother about the game of *Mario Kart* they intend to play this weekend. Elise and Drew are talking about something completely unrelated, but they are equally as engrossed in conversation. I watch, curious, as Elise and Drew laugh at something they're talking about. Drew sips from his glass of wine, nearly choking as his wife continues the joke.

I look away, feeling like I've spied on something I shouldn't have. I know it's silly to think that way, but my decision to be better for this family did not make me immediately part of it. As much as I have not adjusted instantaneously, neither have they. The separation between me and them becomes dreadfully apparent at some moments, but I'm trying not to mind it. We're all learning to be better, after all.

"So has Lavender told you guys about Emerson yet?" Kai says to the table, and I'm thrown so far out of my own head I flinch a little bit.

"What are you talking about?" I ask him, warning in my tone. I flash him a glare that says *shut up!*

He's taken a liking to teasing me regarding this specific topic. I think it's because he likes seeing me completely flustered, and so when he noticed Emerson and I walking in the hallway together a few times, he took to incessant but playful pestering. He always asks who I'm texting, always asks how my "girlfriend" is.

Kai laughs, looking a bit mischievous. "You know exactly what I'm talking about!"

I roll my eyes, my face absolutely burning, and pray the conversation gets dropped. I definitely don't want to talk about this here, or anywhere, *ever.*

"She didn't tell us anything!" Elise says, sounding amused but very interested.

"Lavender has, like, a girlfriend or whatever," Kai says matter-of-factly, but he just sounds like an idiot.

"I absolutely do not! You're so rude!" I drop my fork and narrow my eyes at him.

Kai looks at me with mock surprise, and I try to refrain from rolling my eyes again. "But you do! I see you in school every day!"

"Just because I see her at school means she's my girlfriend? How did you even come to that conclusion? And it isn't *every day*!" I explain, feeling defensive. I know his intentions are pure, but it makes me embarrassed to talk about Emerson like this, like I have a right to.

Now Kai looks a bit confused, as if he hadn't completely thought all of this out. I shake my head, but I'm laughing, too.

"I guess I did assume, but she's still your girlfriend, right?" he asks, spearing an olive with his fork and chewing it thoughtfully.

"No!" I insist. "She's just my... friend, I guess? I don't know, we're basically just acquaintances. I don't even know her last name."

And the truth is, I really have no idea. About her last name, about any of it. I know for a fact I like her—no one could pay me enough money to admit it out loud—but I don't know much else past that. Sure, we had that one random night. And, sure, we have moments in the hallways, stolen conversations in between classes. But that's it.

In some ways, I'm disappointed with the lack of contact since that night. I know it meant more to me than it did to her, and I know my expectations might've been raised a little too high, but... I don't know. I guess I figured if I started living a good life, everything would come to me. I know it's a childish thought, but after a few days of this new journey, I know that isn't the way things work. It isn't magic. I have to work for it.

So maybe Emerson and I will stay acquaintances forever. Who cares? I can't say I'll enjoy it much, but when have I really enjoyed anything?

Stargazing... my brain reminds me, but I shove the memory away. Fine, she was capable of making me enjoy one thing. But what does that matter if I'm not working toward what I truly want, which is a healthy home?

I have to focus on that goal before I can focus on anything else. I've already almost screwed this up entirely. I only have one chance left. As much as I like her, Emerson will not distract me from something this important.

"If she's your friend, why are you so red, huh?" Kai asks. But at this point, after reminding myself how dissatisfied I am with Emerson right now, it's enough.

"I'm red because you embarrassed me, Kai. Can we drop it now, please?" My tone is serious but not rude, and Kai lays off without looking hurt about it.

Did you know you can set boundaries with people without them hating you and wishing for you to go to hell? I've just learned that myself.

Elise chimes in as she lifts her fork to her mouth. "You know, whatever Emerson is right now, she can always come over and you can hang out. Kai and Leia have friends over all the time. Only if you want, of course."

"I don't know," I say hesitantly. "I've never really talked to her about hanging out before. Maybe I will. Thank you."

Elise and Drew look satisfied at my response. I think about it. Is it possible I can have a healthy home *and* a friend? Perhaps so. Even though it seems terrifying, maybe I will ask Emerson. That's a normal thing, right? If I ask her to come over and watch TV or something?

I'll be sure to ask her in the most casual way possible.

* * *

It turns out it's hard to be casual when you're overthinking just how casual you have to be. I don't want her to think I'm asking her out, but I also don't want her to think I'm not interested. Then again, it's always possible she hates me and wants nothing to do with me, in which case she'll be rude no matter how casual I am.

I think about it all night and all morning the next day at school. I usually see Emerson when I'm walking from lunch to English, which is the best time for us to talk since after lunch is the longest passing time we have.

I eagerly await this part of the day, and I'm sorry and embarrassed to say I'm overly excited about the idea of inviting my friend to *my house*. It's so simple to other people, I'm sure, but the prospect of asking her over, inviting her inside, taking her up to my room, showing her my stuff. It's stupid, I know, but it makes me sort of giddy when I think about it.

When the end of lunch rolls around, I'm scolding myself for feeling so nervous. I feel like I'm trying too hard to be normal, to *act* normal, and I'm afraid Emerson will think

I'm weird. But, unfortunately, I don't see Emerson while I'm walking to lunch. I even stand and wait to see if she's running late, but I'm almost late to class, and I have to walk away. I'm mad at myself for feeling disappointed. I know I'll see her in art at the end of the day, but it isn't ideal. She'll be around her friends, and I know her friends don't like me. I don't know if I'll have enough courage to even bring it up around them.

Once art rolls around, I'm on the verge of throwing up over this. It's gotten to the point where I have overthought it too much. Because I just want it over with, I decide I'll walk up to Emerson at the first available opportunity to get it out of the way.

I just don't think through how quickly that opportunity will approach until it's in my face.

Still, I don't allow myself another moment to consider it. In a random moment of boldness, I walk up to Emerson and all of her friends, who sit at the end of the art table in a huddle. Luke notices me first, and he gives me a smile, but he seems a little worried.

"Emerson?" I say. I hope my voice isn't shaking as much as I think it is, but I feel like I've just spoken into a microphone that broadcasted my voice all around the classroom. It makes me feel impossibly tiny.

Emerson turns around, very clearly surprised, and looks at me expectantly.

"Can I talk to you for a second?" I ask.

She looks back at her friends, then at me, and in the back of my head I wonder if she made a face at them, as if trying to make fun of me. But I don't let it bother me.

She gets up slowly and follows me to where I sit, where it's nice and quiet and a little more private. Or, it should be, but the eyes of all Emerson's friends—including Luke—are right on us.

"What's up?" she asks me.

I take a deep breath, then blurt out, "Would you wanna maybe come over tonight? I know it's weird and we're barely friends or anything but I just thought it could be fun, like, we could watch a movie or a show or eat something or... well, I don't care what we do, but... do you wanna come?"

My heart thuds loudly in my chest as Emerson's eyes widen a little bit. I don't know if I've caught her off guard or if she is appalled at my invitation. My stomach sinks as I watch her glance back at her friends, who are snickering. I look down at my ratty sneakers and try not to let it get to me. But I know what she's going to say before she says it.

She lets out a halfhearted chuckle that contains no humor, her expression now reserved. Her tone is flat and halfhearted when she says, "Um, sorry, but I'm busy tonight."

I give her a stiff smile as my mood drops completely, straight to the floor, then deeper, as far down as it can go. "And, I'm sure, you're busy the whole weekend. And every weekend after that. Is that right?"

Emerson looks hurt, but the expression is erased quickly so she doesn't show her plastic friends she's a human being who experiences a whole range of emotions and thoughts. No, that would just be too much for them to handle, wouldn't it?

"Yeah," Emerson says softly. Her heart isn't in it, though. "It is right."

She goes back to sit with her stupid friends so she can talk about me, probably, and I sit down at my own table.

Acquaintances, then? Or should I jump right to best friends?

I sigh, burying my face in my hands. Clearly, Kai and I had the wrong idea about Emerson. Too bad I got my hopes up.

As soon as class begins, I tell the teacher I'm not feeling well, and I wander the halls for the rest of class. Call me crazy, but I don't want Emerson to see me upset over her.

CHAPTER THIRTEEN

On the way home from school, Kai asks me if I've talked Emerson about coming over yet, but I just say no. I think he can tell I'm disappointed about something or other, but I don't feel like talking about it with him right now, or maybe at all. All of this is completely new territory—having someone to talk to—and I'm still not exactly sure how to navigate it. Step by step, I suppose.

When we walk into the house, Kai tells me he's making pancakes for us, including Leia, who should be home in about fifteen minutes. I respond with excitement and head upstairs to drop off my bag and shoes.

My bedroom door stands widely ajar, and as I approach it, I know something's off. Looking inside, my eyes immediately go to the right, where the dresser stands. Both drawers closest to the floor are wide open, and my clothes have been strewn about as if someone went through them. Not only that, but some papers I had lying on the floor for school are crumpled and ripped.

I take a deep breath, shutting my eyes, trying not to let the paranoia creep in, but before I know it, my stomach is churning. My thoughts take off quickly, like a flock of birds when startled. And even though the thoughts are barely distinguishable, I get the gist of what happened.

They're looking through my things, invading my privacy—the Kahales. Trying to find a way to get me out of here? Trying to make me upset? Trying to make me look guilty? Maybe this whole thing has been a setup. Maybe Jacob's on his way right now to see the mess I made in my room. They'll claim I had some sort of breakdown to get me out of here. It was an act? They got me to believe them? How didn't I see this before?

"Hey, you okay?" I hear from behind me, and I turn slowly.

At the doorway stands Kai, nonchalantly, as if he had nothing to do with this. I bet that smile on his face is mocking. I bet he feels no regret for what's happened.

"What is this?" I ask in my scary-calm voice, because if this really is what I think it is, I'm not leaving before they know what they did to me was wrong.

"What's what?" he inquires confusedly. He walks further into the room to see what I see. When he spots the mess, he looks between it and me several times, a deep furrow in his dark brow.

I cross my arms and face him, staring him down scathingly, hating the pretend puzzlement on his face. "So what, you're just gonna pretend like you didn't know about this?"

He jerks back as if I've struck him, eyes widening. "Know about what?"

I gesture around dramatically, pointing out the obvious. "This, Kai! What, are they kicking me out? Are they trying to upset me? Are *you*?"

"You're talking about the mess?"

I sigh, exasperated, growing angrier by the second. Why doesn't he understand? Why can't he just be truthful so this can be over with?

"You think we messed up your room or something? It was the cat, Lavender," he says, as if it's obvious. As if I'm stupid.

I narrow my eyes. "Do you think I'm an idiot?"

He backs up, holding his hands up. "No! I didn't say that! But Hiro does this all the time if I forget to shut my door! I don't know why, he likes getting behind the drawers."

"What?"

"Look, I'd bet he's behind one of them right now."

He walks to the drawers, and I let him because there isn't any further damage he could do if he or his family really is responsible.

Kai kneels to reach the second to last drawer, and behind it, Hiro sleeps contentedly, all four of his paws tucked snugly beneath his gray and white body. But when the light hits him, he gives us a grumpy look and *meows* very angrily, almost like he's telling us to put the drawer back before he kills us.

"Oh," I say, feeling embarrassed. My face and neck heat as the paranoia leaves my brain, my adrenaline shutting down. I really *am* an idiot. "I didn't… I just thought—"

Kai stands, interrupting me hastily. "It's fine, Lavender. Even though I don't understand what you've been through, I understand trust issues. It's hard to not think the worst sometimes. But for what it's worth, we aren't planning on doing anything to you. And you're definitely not getting kicked out. Like, ever."

Before I have a chance to say anything, we hear the front door open as Leia comes home. She yells, asking where we are, and both Kai and I respond equally as loudly, telling her we're in my room.

She comes up in a second. Her backpack still on her shoulders, she comes into my room with a huge smile on her face. "What's up?"

Leia notices the mess, but her face hardly changes. In fact, she lets out a laugh when she says, "Hiro got in here, didn't he?"

I brush my hair back and shrug. "Yeah, I guess he did."

"Are you okay?" Leia asks me.

I sit down on my bed, suddenly feeling very tired. It's strange to go from zero to one hundred, then right back to zero all in a few moments. My brain feels like it's just gone on a rollercoaster.

"Yeah, I'm fine. I don't know why I thought so, but when I saw the mess, I thought you guys had done something. Or your parents."

Leia sits next to me, her nose scrunched up. "Why would we do that?"

I shake my head, laughing humorlessly. "I have no idea, honestly. It's just hard to tell the difference between something my brain makes up and something that's real. I know that probably sounds weird."

But Leia doesn't look weirded out or confused. Neither does Kai, for that matter. He comes and sits on the other side of me, trapping me in like a sandwich.

"I don't think that's weird. Like, sometimes when I'm going upstairs at night, I think there's a ghost following me up the stairs. And when I was a kid I was scared the vacuum would eat me in my sleep."

Kai looks at Leia seriously. "Leia, we all know you're still afraid of the vacuum cleaner."

I try hard not to laugh at that. Leia fights back weakly with, "Am not!"

I cover my mouth as I laugh, feeling bad for Leia but loving I'm in the middle of this.

Kai says, "I think what little sister is trying to say is it isn't weird to have fears. Fears are things our brains make up, aren't they? I mean, being afraid of the dark, or heights, or anything like that. You're scared because of something that could happen that probably won't happen. Your brain just makes you think about that *what if*."

I grow serious, letting his words sink in. He's right, but I'd never thought of it that way before. I never thought other people could relate to this, if I'm being honest. I've never really been vocal about my anxiety or paranoia or whatever, but I guess I am just really, really scared. I've gotten to the point where I expect the worst to happen. I assume it will, and I don't think that's good.

"You're right, Kai," I say, looking at him out of the corner of my eye. "Thanks."

He nods, offering me a smile that makes his eyes even warmer. I try to return it, but I'm afraid it's a bit wobbly. Not because I'm sad, but because I'm... happy. Who would've thought?

"I'll talk to my mom about therapy," Leia says. "I'll see if she found any counseling services yet."

I nod at her thankfully, giving her a quick hug from the side.

The three of us sit in silence for a moment, before Kai interrupts it, rubbing his hands together thoughtfully. "So not trying to ruin the moment or anything, but... pancakes?"

* * *

Because Emerson declined my invitation for tonight, I am fortunately able to say yes once again to a movie. Tonight's movie is family-oriented and animated, and the Kahales are particularly excited because it happens to be one of their favorites, and I haven't seen it before. I find myself becoming just as excited as they are, even though it makes me feel slightly nerdy. Not a bad thing, just a new thing.

I sit on the couch sandwiched between Leia and Kai once more. I find we end up like this basically every night, and sometimes I like to tell myself it's because they both want to sit next to me, but I'm sure it's just a fluke that it happens often. Even still, it boosts my self-confidence, knowing I might just be wanted here.

While Elise and Drew get the popcorn, Leia, Kai, and I keep ourselves entertained with conversation. We're talking about the movie we're about to watch since I know nothing about it, but when that conversation comes to a natural stop, Kai changes the subject.

"So Lavender," he says, trying too hard to sound casual. "Why couldn't Emerson come?"

I feign confusion. "What do you mean? I told you I didn't ask."

Kai looks forward at the television screen, blank at the moment. "Luke told me you did."

I let out an annoyed sigh. "Why is he always in my business?"

"He told me because he felt bad." Kai shrugs, looking concerned. "He said you looked embarrassed and wanted to make sure you're okay."

My building anger fizzles out. I know Luke isn't a bad person, and I shouldn't take it out on him if he really did go to Kai because he wanted to make sure I was okay.

"I am okay," I say truthfully. "I was just surprised, I guess. I didn't think she'd say no."

Leia butts in with, "Wait, this girl told you *no*? She said she didn't want to hang out with you?"

I nod solemnly.

"What's the matter with *her*?"

Kai laughs out loud. "There's nothing wrong with her, but she doesn't like hanging out with people other than her friends. It's dumb high school bullshit."

"Well, why doesn't she?" I ask.

He shrugs. "She's just mean, I guess. I don't know."

But I shake my head. "I don't think that's true. She wasn't mean to me that night. Not once, and never before today."

Kai doesn't have the answers, though. Perhaps there *is* something wrong with Emerson, though. Nothing serious, but maybe she's too worried about other people to do what she wants. Even taking myself out of the equation, who knows if she really likes those people she hangs out with if she's a completely different person around them? I can't imagine how I'd change that, but it still gets me thinking about her and what might be going on with her.

As I sit thinking about it, I notice Kai getting particularly grumpy as the minutes tic by.

"What's the matter?" I ask, annoyed because he won't stop huffing and puffing.

"I'm starving!" He gives me wide eyes as he asks, "Can you go check on the popcorn, please?"

I roll my eyes as I stand. "Yeah, whatever."

Leia and Kai yell their thanks as I walk away, and I wonder comically if this is the only reason I'm around.

The kitchen smells strongly of buttery popcorn, but I don't see it on the counter or in the microwave. I don't see Elise and Drew, either, so I walk further into the kitchen, closer to the connecting den.

Elise and Drew are standing there, half in the kitchen, half in the den. They don't know I'm there, so their overly-tense conversation continues. I haven't a clue what they're talking about, but it seems serious. Though I feel like an intruder in someone else's home, I can't look away. What if it's about me? What if there's something wrong? Even so, what if it *isn't* about me? It's possible families can have issues unrelated to their scruffy foster kid, and the idea of a separate issue makes me nervous too, more for Kai and Leia than myself.

I debate walking away, but Elise holds the popcorn bowl, and I told Kai I'd go and check on it, so he'll expect me to come back with it. I hesitate for several moments, listening to the hushed tones, and my heart drops when I hear my name.

Before I can think it through, I blurt, "What's going on?"

They both jump, looking at me with shock and embarrassment written on their faces.

"Are you guys okay?" I ask when they don't reply.

"Yes, of course, honey. Everything's fine," Elise assures me. Her eyes are focused on her fidgeting hands rather than me. "We'll be right over with the popcorn, all right?"

I nod, turn, and walk away, but I feel separated from my body as I recount what just happened. I try so hard not to let the memory of that conversation consume me, but it's nearly impossible. I can't help being terrified of those *what-ifs*, wondering if Elise and Drew are having second thoughts. Wondering if Elise and Drew have decided to get rid of me.

CHAPTER FOURTEEN

The bustling students are muted as I walk through the crowded hallway, Kai's earbuds pressed firmly into my ears. The music that plays is loud and blocks everything, from every direction, just the way I like it. Today it's Duran Duran.

Kai has still been feeling bad about what Emerson did to me, so he offered his headphones up again today. I gratefully accepted because I knew it would get me through the day, and it's like I've traveled to paradise. It's interesting how less scary this school becomes when it's utterly silent around me. Just my music and me.

I'm concentrating on a guitar riff as I walk to my first class, feeling like I am in my own bubble. My mind is so narrowed it gives me tunnel vision, and I don't notice when Luke approaches me from the front. Somehow, I end up plowing right through him.

I take the earbuds out immediately, an apology falling from my lips.

"Damn, Lavender!" he exclaims, clutching his stomach where I accidentally elbowed him.

"I'm sorry! I wasn't paying attention!"

Luke laughs breathlessly. "Your expression was so intense! It looked like you were walking to a battlefield or something. You good?"

"Yes, I'm fine. I was just… lost in thought," I reassure him, laughing softly.

I expect to just walk away now, as in, conversation over. But Luke gestures to the side of the hallway so we can talk out of the way from those trying to walk. I follow him begrudgingly, because it's not every day he tries to talk to me, so maybe it's important.

"You haven't spoken to Emerson recently, right?" he asks, seeming casual enough. He leans against the lockers, running a hand through his blond hair.

I'm not surprised he's asking, since he only really talks to me when it's about Emerson, so I say, "No, I haven't. Why?"

"Meet her in the gym during lunch. Okay?"

I narrow my eyes, confused. "What? Why would I do that?"

Luke shakes his head. "Emerson just told me to tell you that." He shrugs as if he doesn't have any other information, which is frustrating.

Crossing my arms, I huff out a sigh. "And why couldn't she tell me herself?"

"I have no idea. It's up to you whether you want to go or not. I'm just the messenger."

"Fine," I breathe, wanting him to just go away. Nothing against Luke, but our conversations—however brief—never tend to put me in a good mood.

Luke and I part ways after stiff goodbyes. I put my earbuds back in, blocking the world out, and wonder what the hell I'm supposed to do about this girl.

* * *

When the bell rings for lunch, I take my sweet time packing up my books and walking down to the gym. I'll admit, I'm upset with the situation Emerson has put me in. She got me to like her and made me think we were friends and now she's acting like we're strangers. I'm not too excited to see what she'll have to say, but I'm too curious to *not* go. I'm sure it will be something hurtful, and even if it isn't, I feel like I won't like it.

I walk into the musty gym with what I hope is a cold expression on my face so no one bothers me or looks at me. Students bustle out in clusters, laughing, talking, and playing music absurdly loud. The polished wood floors make my sneakers squeak, and the stink of rubber and sweat overcomes me. You'd think I'd be used to the smell of a high school gym at this point, but it seems to get worse as I get older.

I look around for Emerson briefly and don't see her, but I notice she's jogging toward me with a huge smile on her face. I don't return it.

"Hey!" she greets me when she arrives, breathing hard. She gestures for me to wait while she catches her breath. "Jeez, this gym is huge! I've never run in my life."

I think she expects me to laugh, but I do no such thing. I merely stand there, arms crossed, waiting for her to say what she needs to say.

"Are you okay?" she asks, concern on her adorable face. Today, her cheeks are flushed a bright pink, but she doesn't wear any pink clothes for a change. Instead, she wears a light blue sweater and baggy jeans.

"Fine," I snap, trying not to get too caught up on the fact she looks beautiful because I hate that she does. It's annoying. How could she do this to me?

Emerson matches my stance, crossing her arms over her chest and pouting. "Come on, Lavender, what's the matter?"

"Why did we have to meet here, Emerson? Why not in the cafeteria or the library, where people eat during lunch?" I ask, nearly snapping at her. I don't really mean to, but I can't deny what I'm feeling, can't deny she isn't making me feel good about myself right now.

She looks away shamefully, down at her battered sneakers. They are the only thing unpolished about her, and she wears them every day. They look almost identical to mine.

"That's what's the matter," I say quietly. "What, are you embarrassed by me or something? Is that what it is?"

She recoils as if I've tried to hit her and furrows her brow. "What? No, of course, I'm not embarrassed. I couldn't care less what everyone else thinks—"

"Emerson." I smile knowingly, my face softening. It isn't that I'm not upset about it anymore, but I'm beginning to understand her problem, maybe even more than she understands it. "You *do* care what everyone else thinks."

"No I don't," she insists, her voice stubborn.

"Fine," I give in, spreading my hands in defeat. "Then what is it?"

She sighs, clearly frustrated, and tugs on a strand of smooth auburn hair. She looks pained, as if she doesn't want to say what she's about to say. I think of telling her to forget it, but I realize I don't want to forget it. I want to understand. I want her to feel like she can tell me, as selfish as that may be.

"I just—I don't know how to do this. I really don't. And I know I messed up because I wanted to hang out with you on Friday so bad and I felt guilty for every second I wasn't there. I just felt so much pressure. I know my friends suck, but I'm caught between this need for friends whether they suck or not and this need to be independent. Before I met you, I had nothing to make me *want* to be independent and do my own thing. I just feel trapped."

And just like that, *I* feel guilty. Where do I get off thinking she's perfect and has no problems of her own? I know about all the issues with her family, and still, some part of me felt like she had no excuse to treat me wrong. I know I haven't been thinking of her in a fair way.

"I'm sorry you feel that way," I say genuinely. "I just didn't know. I thought maybe you weren't interested and I was just being weird. But I understand now I didn't get the whole picture, and I'm sorry for that."

Emerson shakes her head slowly, looking troubled. "You have no reason to apologize. I was a jerk."

I laugh softly. "You were, but I forgive you."

"Thanks."

"I think we need to work on our communication," I admit. "And if you ever need help feeling not-trapped, just let me know."

She nods, a small smile on her face, and looks relieved. I'm relieved, too. I didn't realize before this how much it was bothering me, but now it's resolved, I feel a lot better. Lighter, almost.

"Thank you. And I agree about the communication thing. We'll talk more, I promise."

After she says it, I feel butterflies in my stomach for no particular reason at all.

Emerson continues, "On that note, do you wanna come with me to a party this weekend?"

"A party?" I repeat, wondering if I've heard her correctly. "You mean, like, a high-school party?"

Emerson laughs. "Yeah, I guess so. Wanna come?"

"Oh." I think frantically of something to say to get out of it, but I remember what we just talked about. "Honestly, I don't really think I'd be comfortable at something like that. I'm sorry."

Emerson looks disappointed but not angry. After a moment, though, she shrugs, apparently forgetting about it. "That's fine. How about I come over and watch a movie, like you said last week?"

I feel that same excitement from last time rising inside me hesitantly. I will it away until I have confirmation. "Really?"

Emerson looks confused. "Of course! I'd love that."

"Okay. Um, that would be great. How's, like, six o'clock? Or seven? Honestly, whenever you want—"

"I'll be at your house at six. Okay?"

I try to suppress the huge grin that threatens to show. I can't let her see how excited I am. Maybe she'll think I'm weird for being so excited. Maybe she isn't even looking forward to this. It isn't a big deal, but all I want to do is squeal and jump. Ugh.

"Yeah, sounds good," I say in a forced-calm voice. Emerson just giggles.

"Cafeteria?" she asks, and if I hadn't been shocked a moment ago, I would be doubly shocked right now.

But I nod and follow her out of the gym, straight to the cafeteria. And we find a table together, just for the two of us, and eat lunch.

* * *

"I know you did not just cut me off, Kai. I know you didn't," Leia demands angrily, fidgeting in her spot on the couch as she presses furiously on her controller's buttons.

"I literally did," Kai said. "I'm about to be in first place. So. Essentially I'm the best player of this game, in the entire world."

Leia grunts furiously. "You are *not*! I'm never playing this with you again."

She sighs dramatically as Kai comes in first place, whooping loudly and standing up. He throws his hands in the air as if he's just won the Superbowl, jumping up and down with glee.

I watch curiously with a smile resting on my face. Call me weird, but I love watching them be siblings. It's so interesting, the dynamic they have. I want to be a part of it, too. And I'm sure they'd say I already am, but I know I'm not yet. I mean, it's only been a few weeks since we met, so there's no way I'm their sister already. I suppose it's just something I'm excited for in the future.

As Kai sits down, his happy dance over with, he asks Leia, "Okay, we playing another one or what?"

"Yep," Leia says, already starting up another game.

This has already happened four times. I don't know how they aren't sick of it yet, but I guess I'm not either. It's hilarious, and I am entertained.

Since Elise and Drew both happened to be working late tonight, the three of us all got our homework done early so we could have the night for goofing off. Kai and I made macaroni and cheese—which was good, but not nearly as good as Emerson's—and chicken nuggets while Leia prepped some pre-made cookie dough for the oven. I can honestly say I've never had this much fun in my life, but I can't admit it out loud. It would sound so lame. I'm sure these kids have been to Disney World, and they'd think *this* is the least fun they've had.

But I don't care. I'm easily pleased, I really am, and I'm enjoying myself. I'm building up the courage to ask for a chance to play *Mario Kart*, but because I've never played it, they'll have to teach me, and I don't want to interrupt their fun. Every round, I tell myself I'll ask to join, but I chicken out.

After the next round, Leia loses again, then asks if I want to play for once. I look at her with uncertainty.

"I've never played this before. I don't know how," I admit.

Both of their jaws drop. They've never looked more alike than they do right now. I can't help but laugh.

"That's tragic," Leia says, putting a hand to her chest for drama purposes. "Kai, put a controller in her hand right now."

And he does. And he teaches me how to play. He's a patient, helpful teacher—perhaps because he's teaching a video game—and I pick it up quickly. Maybe *too* quickly; I end up beating Kai in our first game together and he has to leave the room.

Leia and I laugh so hard our stomachs hurt, and we can't breathe at some point. As we're clutching our chests, we hear the front door open and try to recollect ourselves.

"Hey, Mom," Leia says to Elise as she walks in.

When I turn to greet her and Drew, my smile fades quickly, the laughter drying in my throat. Elise looks stressed. Not just stressed, maybe even panicked, scared. And Drew, walking in behind her, doesn't look so far off. It unsettles my stomach, and I feel the mac n' cheese and chicken nuggets churning in there.

Leia is the first to ask, "What's wrong?"

She does so just as Kai is walking back in. Though his ego is very clearly bruised, he looks happy to greet his parents... until he sees their faces. I'm glad I'm not the only one noticing it.

Elise puts on a fake smile. "Everything's fine! Just a long workday. For me and your father."

Leia, Kai, and I all look at each other, as if trying to speak to each other with our eyes. I can tell no one else is buying it even a little bit.

"Are you sure?" Kai presses, walking closer to them. "You both seem upset."

Drew looks at his son and forces a smile too. "Like Mom said, it's just been a hard workday. But really, everything's good."

"Okay," Kai says uncertainly. "You'd tell us if it wasn't, right?"

"Of course," Elise promises. I feel a tightness in my chest, a cold feeling that spreads from my stomach outward. "By the way, Leia and Lavender, you both have therapy appointments this Thursday at 4 p.m. All right?"

It goes over my head completely, and I nod my head absently. I can tell Leia's doing the same when she gives me a concerned look. But Elise and Drew don't speak on it for the rest of the night. In fact, they don't say much of anything. I can't help but feel like something bad is about to happen.

CHAPTER FIFTEEN

Elise and Drew act strange for the next couple of days. They're still wonderful and kind, but the three of us kids can guess that something is very wrong. Leia, Kai, and I have been discussing it before bed for the past couple nights, gathering in my bedroom for around an hour each night. I can tell we're all stressed, but I think it's specifically taking its toll on Leia. I don't think this family ever had secrets before I came along, which is what makes me think it's likely about me.

I don't want to assume this, however, because I know it's a dangerous thought process. If I go down that road, I might not ever come back from it. But I also don't want something separate from me to be the issue. Leia and Kai have ruled out a death in the family because an uncle of theirs had passed away a few years ago, and it wasn't like this at all. I hope no one's actually dead, but I personally do not take the possibility off the table. It could be different this time.

We have considered that maybe one of them got laid off at work. Divorce has been brought up, but Leia almost heaved at the prospect, so Kai and I shut that one down immediately.

What none of us has said out loud is, what if they're sending me away?

I don't know if the two of them have had this thought because they clearly know their own parents better than I do. It's still all I can think about, however. Maybe it's too much for them to have a third kid in the house right now. Maybe it's financial difficulties, or maybe they just don't think I'm getting on well here. Maybe it was the therapy that bumped up my expenses. Whatever it is, it's freaking me out.

The only thing that's able to take my mind off of it all is, surprisingly, spending time with Emerson.

She's been a lot more present as my friend lately, which I really like. I understand that sometimes she wants me to leave her alone, and I do, but for the most part, we're a lot more friendly than before. I know it isn't the best possible situation, but what I do know is that Emerson has established boundaries for herself. They may not make sense to me, but they sure do make sense to her. And until I'm closer to her, I cannot infiltrate those boundaries. I have to let her come to me, and forcing my way in will not make her feel comfortable enough to do that.

So, we walk to class together in the morning. We spend some time at lunch together, and walk to class after that. And in art, we wave, but I leave her alone and let her talk to her other friends. I'm okay with it, really. It makes such a difference to have someone to talk to in school at all, so I don't mind leaving her be after our designated time.

Plus, we text *all* the time, which is also brand new to me. We talk about nothing sometimes, but other times we talk about our lives. She tells me about the latest thing her parents said or did, and I tell her about something funny Leia said to me.

Sometimes we even talk about more personal things; Emerson about how her parents were absent during her childhood, and me about my birth parents. She's particularly been interested in why I have no interest in meeting them, but, as I've explained to others who have asked, I have no interest in meeting the people who had a hand in delivering me to this life. I get it, circumstance probably screwed my mom over, but I think I'll always feel some resentment toward her for giving me up, whether it's fair or not. It's *my* life, *my* trauma, and I don't think I should want to meet her or my dad if it doesn't appeal to me.

It feels really good to say this stuff to someone after years of repressing it. I don't know what it is exactly that makes it so easy to talk to Emerson. She never pries but always lets me know she's there. But she *always* asks, never seems uninterested. She has found the perfect way to support me as a friend I didn't even realize I needed in my life. I know it isn't anything like therapy to have a friend to talk to, but I imagine it might feel similar. I can only hope that Emerson feels the same about me so far. Although, I don't know how to be a friend, really. It's never really occurred to me to learn. I think I'm doing all right for my first time.

The only thing about Emerson that has been striking my curiosity is the way in which she stops answering at the same time every night. I know, I know—she probably goes to sleep. But something about it just gives me a funny feeling.

Every night at around nine, Emerson will stop replying but will continue the conversation very early the next morning, before I'm even awake. I asked her if she goes to bed early, and she said, "Not really." It's not that I care much, I just hope she's okay. I hope she isn't breaking down every night or doing something stupid. Some tiny part of me also thinks Emerson might be sick of me already—meaning I'm not doing as well as I think I am—but I try not to think about it too hard.

On Thursday afternoon, Emerson and I sit at our usual lunch table, which is in a secluded spot of the cafeteria located all the way at the back near some floor-to-ceiling windows. They let in the watery late November daylight that clashes horribly with the blinding fluorescent lights that will never not be dizzying. There are about ten minutes left before the bell will ring, telling us to go to our next class and continue on with our day.

"Did I tell you I'm going to therapy for the first time today?" I ask casually, sipping my water.

Emerson shakes her head. "No, you didn't. Are you scared?"

"Not really. I'm a little nervous, I guess, but I think it will be good for me. What do you think?"

She shrugs as she finishes off her granola bar. It's vegan and looks like dirt, but it smells like blueberries. "I think it will be good for you, too."

"Well, have you ever been to a therapist before?" I inquire, mostly just because I'm curious. I know Emerson had mentioned struggling with mental health in the past, but who knows if her parents ever cared enough to send her to therapy?

Emerson looks away, clearly avoiding my eyes. I wish I never brought it up, suddenly, and I'm struck with the realization that I still don't know Emerson as well as I think I do. Sure, she shares some things about her life, but there have to be things she leaves out. I suppose I've left out things, too, so it's only fair. But it still makes me curious.

I just want to *know* her. I never knew how frustrating it was to *get* to know someone before. I don't think I've ever wanted to before. But there is such a strong urge inside of me to know her entire life story, so *I* could be the person she calls when she's upset, the person she relies on and trusts wholeheartedly. But we have a long way to go until then, if that ever even is to happen.

Often I wonder if she feels this way too, because I would feel embarrassed if she didn't. I'm frightened by this *want* inside of me. This want that drives me nuts, to just know everything there is to know about Emerson. To be friends. Right? Just friends.

"I'm sorry for bringing it up," I say. "I shouldn't have."

"Oh, no, it's okay," Emerson dismisses. But she does not elaborate any further, and it seems clear I've struck a nerve. So I don't pry.

* * *

I sit in the backseat with Leia, who's vibrating with nerves. I silently hold my hand out for her to take it, and she does, squeezing the life out of it.

"It's okay. I promise," I say quietly.

I feel bad. I can't imagine how terrified she must be right now. I know she has struggles when it comes to meeting new people, but who knows what else she's struggling with that she hasn't even opened up to me about? From the way anxiety has worked in my own brain, I know her adrenaline is running a mile a minute. I wish I knew how to calm her down, to actually reassure her.

"Look at me," I try. I'm taken back to that night with Emerson in her car and how she was able to make me feel so calm so quickly. Even if it doesn't help Leia in the same way, I should attempt it, shouldn't I? "Do you want to breathe with me for a minute?"

My heart aches at the memory those words bring back, but I fight through it. Leia looks at me with uncertainty and nods.

While our eyes are locked, I breathe in as deeply as possible and watch as Leia does the same. I give her an encouraging smile and hope in the back of my mind that this is helping in any sort of way. It helped me when Emerson did it.

We take five good, deep breaths, and Leia thanks me and goes back to looking out the window. Though I'm sure she's still nervous, I think she's stopped shaking, so that counts for something, right?

When we get to the office, Elise, Leia, and I walk in together. The office looks standard; the floors are covered with brown, stiff carpeting and the walls are painted white. It's boring, but the place is clean and smells like cinnamon. At the smell, I immediately think of Emerson, but know that I can't start thinking about her right now because I need to focus on myself for this to work.

Elise checks both of us in at the front desk, and we're told to sit in the waiting room until our therapists are ready for us. Leia's comes out first, but Leia insists that her mom goes in with her. The therapist seems fine with it, and I watch as they walk down the hallway. I'm sure it's normal for that to happen, but I do think Leia might benefit from doing it alone at some point. There might always be a filter on when her mom is around, not because Elise would be judgmental, but because Elise is her mom. Leia might feel more comfortable saying things to her therapist without her around.

It isn't long before my own therapist comes out to greet me. She introduces herself as Cristina and shakes my hand. Her grip is firm but soft, her face warm and open. She wears a soft purple sweater and gray dress pants, and her kind brown eyes look at me in a way that tells me she is genuine, that maybe I can trust her.

"Nice to meet you," I say. "I'm Lavender."

"Nice to meet you too!" she responds excitedly. Cristina smiles with her whole face, not just her mouth, if that makes sense. I can tell she probably smiles easily. "You can just follow me right this way to my office, alright, Lavender?"

I nod and follow her down the brightly-lit hallway to her office. It has a comfy-looking red couch in front of a desk, which has a computer on it. Through a small window on the far wall, the watery fall sunshine peeks, making everything look a little gray. But the office is comfortable and cozy, and I sit down on the couch across from Cristina.

Immediately, I get lost in the talking. Cristina asks me some routine questions, and then we get into my life. She's such a good listener, I feel like I'm talking to Emerson, but it is still different than talking to her or anyone else. I can tell Cristina is analyzing my words and me the moment they meet the air, and even though it doesn't bother me, it's definitely different.

When I get to mentioning Emerson—considering she's all I think about these days—Cristina gives me a comforting smile. I find myself wanting Cristina to ask more questions about Emerson and me so I can answer them and keep talking and talking, but she doesn't ask much of anything. Instead, she lets me babble and babble until I strike something that she wants to focus on. Some of these focal points include my biological parents, the age I was when I was admitted into the system, my time so far at the Kahales. You know, the boring stuff—the stuff that actually might be causing me some serious trauma.

She doesn't give me *much* advice, but what she does do is tell me that I'm in the right place, that a lot of foster children end up in therapy due to general mistreatment. She also says that children who haven't met their birth parents can suffer from trauma they don't even realize they have, and maybe that's why I resent my parents so much.

I don't agree with that viewpoint on my relationship with my parents entirely, mostly because I've conditioned myself to believe one thing for my whole life. But I tell myself that she's the expert, so I should probably listen to her.

The appointment as a whole feels like a very positive experience, which is something new. I always thought that attending a therapy session would feel a lot like being in a glass jar, but I didn't at all. I felt comfortable, more comfortable than I thought possible. And even though I was hesitant to open up, Cristina makes me feel okay about it.

She leaves me with one final message, which is that she is looking forward to talk to me again next time, and then I am dismissed.

When I get out, I sit in the waiting room since it seems like Elise and Leia haven't come out yet. When they do, Leia sees me and immediately hugs me tight.

"What was that for?" I ask, surprised but not upset.

Leia just shakes her head and gives me a grateful smile. "Thank you for coming with me. I already feel good about this."

I return her smile and feel like crying. "Of course."

Once at home, we eat dinner with Kai and Drew. Both are eager to know some details about Leia's experience. They don't ask anything personal, but they want to know if Leia feels like this will be good for her, and Leia seems lighter and happier than I've ever seen her. I don't know what was said in her appointment, but whatever it was, it seems like she could be getting some help that she really, really deserves.

The entire family is so unbelievably happy for her. Kai ruffles her hair, Leia laughs and shoves his hand away, and Drew makes sure Leia knows they're all there for her through this.

Later that night, I'm feeling warm and cozy, filled to the brim with sushi and green salad. In my happy mood, I decide that I want to call Emerson so I can tell her about tonight. We've spoken on the phone a few times before, always instigated by her, but I'm feeling bold, wondering how she is and what she did tonight.

As the phone rings, I pluck at a loose thread on my blanket. I'm nervous I might be overstepping her boundaries by calling like this, but then she picks up.

"Lavender! Hi!" she says loudly. The background noise is deafening.

"Emerson? Where are you?"

I hear her laugh and respond to someone else, saying things I cannot understand, her words drawn out and slurred. "Oh! I'm—I forget, honestly!"

She erupts into another fit of giggles, and I feel a coldness spread over my skin, goosebumps forming in its wake.

"Are you all right?" I ask, but it feels like I'm screaming into an empty void. Emerson either cannot hear anything I'm saying, or she's choosing to ignore me.

"Emerson, are you there?" I try, but again, no response. Just giggles and more slurred words that I cannot decipher.

Finally, I hang up the phone in frustration and confusion. It probably isn't any of my business, really, but she was drunk, right? I try racking my brain for any instance where I've met a drunk person. I haven't really, only seen them on television, but she was acting like she was drunk or high or something. Again, none of my business, but it worries me a little bit. I mean, it's a Thursday night... why is she partying?

Though it isn't fair, it keeps me up all night.

CHAPTER SIXTEEN

When I was twelve, I was shipped off to a foster home mere days after my birthday. It was nearing Christmastime and snow flurries floated around the city streets amongst the honking of cars and the distant sirens. My new foster home was very much removed from the chaos of the city, which I liked, but that was just about where the list of things I liked here ended.

The street was piled high with garbage, which isn't uncommon for the city, but it seemed like the trash piles made the street smaller and more cluttered. The air smelled of rotting food, and I somehow knew rats were running rampant all along the sidewalks, even though I never saw them.

At the time, I was being hauled around by a social worker named Amanda, who had not one apologetic bone in her body. She treated her job like a *job*, and I knew from day one it wasn't the job she even wanted. She sighed when I put my trash bag of stuff in her car and sighed when I took it out—"It's just so unsanitary!" No matter how many times I explained there wasn't ever any trash in it, she thought it was unladylike for me to carry around my belongings in a trash bag. One time, I told her to buy me a backpack or shove it. And what do you know? She actually bought me a backpack.

I walked up to the stoop of my new foster home, freshly twelve, with a brand new backpack slung across my right shoulder. I stared up at the black metal bars that seemed to guard my new house and listened to the doorbell buzz like flies on a hot day. In the doorway appeared a nasty man, a limp toupee resting on his very obviously bald head. The door opened with a gust of stale air, and when he smiled, I looked down at my shoes so I didn't barf. In the simplest of terms, Mr. Yarrow knew very little about hygiene, but he was supposedly one of the "best foster parents the system had" according to Amanda. And when I heard that, I thought, *I wouldn't want to see the worst of them.*

Mr. Yarrow had a wife, Mrs. Yarrow, who was much too pretty for a man like her husband. She wasn't supermodel pretty, but she was pretty in her own way. Mrs. Yarrow was at least five years younger than her husband and twice as tall. She had a kind smile and round blue eyes. I remember thinking this place might not be so bad, and I settled into my life at the Yarrows' place fairly quickly after Amanda left.

The Yarrows had no children of their own but had three other foster children, all of which were little boys. I didn't get on much with them because of the age gap, but I thanked them often in my head for being boys, because it meant I had a room of my very own.

For four nights, I stayed at the Yarrow residence without an incident. It wasn't a five-star experience, but I had warm food every night and a bed without bugs. They didn't use harsh punishments like spanking or cold showers, didn't yell unless it was solicited, and for the most part, we kids only dealt with Mrs. Yarrow.

Mrs. Yarrow took a special liking to me, though. She talked to me a lot, about all kinds of things, most of which I didn't fully understand. Really I just listened in silence and thanked her whenever she would remind me about how beautiful I was, which was very often. She told me I looked like her when she was young and she wanted me to be her very own daughter, but Mr. Yarrow would never allow it. She talked lots and lots about infertility—a word I didn't know at the time—and about how she'd have a million children if Mr. Yarrow *wasn't* infertile.

But the gist of Mrs. Yarrow's babbling was she wanted me and wanted to be my mother. She wanted me to be her little girl, and I wanted more than anything to be just that. This place wasn't perfect by any means, but it had to do because I was getting old and the older I got, Amanda always told me, the harder it was to find someone who really wanted me.

In my twelve-year-old brain, I composed a scheme to get Mr. Yarrow to begin to like me. No, not lik*e—adore*. Mr. Yarrow would like me so much he would want to sign adoption papers as soon as possible, and soon, this would be my real home. I'd have an address, a school that was just mine, friends, a mom and a dad, and even though the house was musty and the street was trashed, it would belong to me.

Mrs. Yarrow always told us kids never to leave our rooms after ten o'clock at night. We were to be well into sleep by then, but we weren't to use the bathroom until the next morning at eight. If it was an emergency, she said, we could knock on our doors to get her attention. But otherwise, we should stay put. She said it was because Mr. Yarrow got terrible, terrible headaches, and he liked to spend time alone, in the quiet.

My plan was to essentially break this rule. After all, I was Mrs. Yarrow's favorite. She would let me break this rule. She'd let me break any rule if she were my mother. So even though I was terrified of leaving my room, and even though the house smelled of skunk, and even though Mr. Yarrow's booming voice often made me tremble, I opened my door one early morning, around six, to trek to the kitchen. I would fetch a glass of water and bring it to Mr. Yarrow, ever the helpful child, and I'd even ask if he needed anything else.

I wasn't even to the kitchen when I knew I'd made a mistake.

The house was hazy and filled with a sharp, sour smell amongst the pungent skunk odor I couldn't place. It was almost pitch black in the hallway, and I kept my hand along the wall to make sure I was going in the right direction. All blinds were drawn shut tightly, and the only sound I could hear was the shuddering snores that were so loud I jumped, lost my footing, and collapsed to the floor in a heap, my ankle caught on some sort of wire. After me fell a lamp, and when I heard the bulb shatter, I felt my heart shatter, too.

The last thing I remember before my memory blacks out is Mr. Yarrow jumping up, clutching his poor, bald head, exclaiming, "*Shut up! It's too loud! My head!*"

In hindsight, I know what happened that day like I know the back of my hand. Old Mr. Yarrow was a lazy drunk, and his wife supported his addiction—probably out of fear—by forcing us kids into our bedrooms. He was hungover that morning and *angry*. In the moment, I thought I was unfazed by the events, but whenever I look back on it, I remember how scared I was and how disgusting I felt, how violated and betrayed by the fact, not only was I not going to be their daughter, but it dawned on me I probably wouldn't *ever* have been their daughter. The concept of alcohol, therefore, left a bad taste in my mouth.

This is all I can think of the next morning when I see Emerson.

"God, my head *kills*. It's way too loud in here," she says, and I flinch because I'm suddenly in a dingy room with a man who reeks of weed.

I look up at her, away from my locker, and I can feel my hardened expression, but I can't bring myself to soften it. I can't pretend I don't feel uncomfortable, but I know I have to. It isn't her fault I've seen what I've seen.

She forces a smile at me, through her supposed headache, but her skin is pale and dark circles are stark against the pallor. I'm thinking to myself, *Has Emerson looked like this before?* And I'm thoroughly afraid, thinking maybe she's been getting drunk like this and I never even realized it. Had I been so caught up in other things I didn't even realize something might be going on with her? What am I, still twelve? Shouldn't I have learned the signs by now?

I reassure myself by remembering I'm only just getting to know her. Perhaps this is just her way of having fun. Perhaps she just likes to go to parties, perhaps I'm overreacting. Tons of teenagers have the same hobby. But I already feel like a shitty friend for not picking up on this before.

"You all right?" I ask, waiting to see if she'll bring it up on her own.

But she only looks at me with confusion. "Of course. Why do you ask?"

I shrug and start walking. She joins me on my right as she fiddles around with her phone. "I don't know. You look like you had a rough night."

She furrows her brow and looks me in the eyes confusedly. "What?"

"Emerson, you're hungover," I blurt out. Accidentally, of course. Because I *know* this isn't my business and shouldn't worry me. But something about her playing it off *does* worry me.

"Why would you even care if I was?" she shoots back, and I can tell she's getting defensive.

"I don't know, I just—it seems like an irresponsible thing to do. Drinking on a school night," I say hesitantly.

She stops walking entirely, widening her eyes at me. I've struck something. "Oh, so now you're calling me *irresponsible*?"

I sigh and cross my arms, running my fingers through my knotty hair I forgot to brush this morning. "I didn't mean to. It came out wrong. I'm worried about you, is all. I just want you to be safe."

"I am," she states matter-of-factly.

"Are you sure?"

"Yes. Now please, can we stop talking about this?"

I hesitate but nod. After all, it's her life. If she wants to get drunk on Thursdays and come to school hungover, that's her prerogative.

But in the back of my mind, I can't help thinking I might have a right to worry. I mean, if we're going to be friends, I'm allowed to be concerned for my friend, right? And all of the little pieces Emerson has introduced me to about her life seem to be adding up in an unsettling way. She told me she's had a problem with suicidal thoughts in the past, and even if that isn't still happening, maybe she's still struggling with depression, or something else. And when I brought up going to a therapist, she *also* got defensive as if she didn't want to talk about it because... because why? She hates therapists? She's embarrassed because she sees one? There could be a myriad of reasons why, and something tells me it probably has to do with her family.

I mean, they're obviously the root of all of her issues. I'd never say it to her, but she has real problems with her parents anyone could see. The only problem is, do I say something about all of this? Or perhaps let her suffer in silence?

"Will you still be coming over tonight?" I ask to change the subject. I can't think about this right now.

Emerson nods. "Definitely. I'm excited!"

"Good! I'm excited too." After a beat of silence, I add, "Will you still feel like this tonight? Or will it go away?"

Emerson laughs lightly. "You've never been hungover, have you?"

I shake my head, as if it wasn't obvious before.

"Oh, Lavender. Your innocence amuses me."

I don't have the heart to point out her irony.

* * *

Despite the complications, I'm more than thrilled Emerson's coming over tonight. In a lot of ways, it feels like I'm starting to have a stable life with people who care about me all around, and hanging out with Emerson is just that next step to achieving further stability.

The Kahales are entertained by my excitement. Kai teases me because he suspects Emerson and I like each other. Leia eventually picks up on this and starts teasing me, too, but it's all in good fun. The teasing only makes me a part of the family, I think, and it fills me with more joy than I could put into words. Elise prepares some snacks for Emerson and I and forces Kai to let me borrow his laptop so we can watch a movie. He wasn't *that* upset about it and I could tell he was excited for me which outweighed any annoyance he may have felt.

As it nears six o'clock at night, I start getting really nervous. What if Emerson gets bored? What if I like her more than she likes me, or what if I made this sound like a date but it isn't really a date? Or worse, what if Emerson thinks this is a date but I have no idea?

Even though Emerson and I had the communication discussion, we never really talked about dating at all. Sure, we made it clear to each other we like girls, but that was it. I wonder if I should make it clear I like her so something can happen, but I don't even know if that's what I want. Everything just seems a little confusing and overwhelming since we're still learning about each other, but that's okay, right? It's normal to feel like this when getting to know someone, especially when you're crushing on them.

I hope that's true.

When I'm all done freaking out and pacing around the house, I sit on the couch to calm my nerves, which doesn't work at all. Leia keeps laughing at me and telling me I look like I'm about to be sick. Kai agrees and asks me if I want a Xanax, which makes Leia get serious.

"Kai, are you offering her drugs right now?" Leia asks dubiously, staring up at her brother with narrowed eyes.

"I was just kidding," he says. "I don't even *have* Xanax. That's just something you say, you know, when someone is stressed—"

"No one says that, you huge idiot." They turn to face each other like they're about to have a brawl, tones firm but playful underneath.

"What do you mean? Of course, they do!" Leia facepalms and shakes her head, listening to Kai ramble on about how people *do* say that, and he *isn't* a drug dealer, but he stops abruptly when the doorbell rings.

My eyes widen and I feel suddenly like I might collapse. My voice shaking, I stammer, "Oh, God, she's here. This is the worst decision I've ever made."

Kai furrows his brow. "Worse than when you decided to run away because we're too *nice*?"

I narrow my eyes and scoff. "Too soon, you *huge idiot*."

Walking to the front door, a million negative thoughts and feelings rush through my brain like it's on overdrive, and

I can't stop asking myself what-if questions. As if a million bees are swarming in my head, I almost can't hear anything, but then I'm opening the door, and there stands Emerson, and the buzzing stops. Silence.

She smiles broadly, giving me a childlike wave. Her hair is up in a messy bun that looks knotted. She wears those pink sweatpants she has with a cream sweater that hangs off one shoulder.

"Hey!" she says enthusiastically, and I can't remember what I was so nervous about.

"Hi," I say softly, biting the inside of my cheek so I don't show how happy I am. "Come in."

I step aside as she walks in, and she does so with that same smile on her face. I wonder if she's amused by me or if she's feeling what I'm feeling. I hope it's the latter.

"It feels weird being back here," she says, looking around.

"You've been here before?"

"Of course! Kai and I used to be close friends," she explains.

As she's saying it, I remember the story Kai told about her at the diner when I first arrived here. I'd almost forgotten how Kai felt about Emerson, and I wonder if he has any thoughts on me hanging out with her, but he's never mentioned anything. "Right. I didn't think of that."

She shrugs but keeps looking around like she's seeing something brand new. "I've always loved it here. It's so much homier than my house. When we were really little, we were allowed to have sleepovers with each other, and I always wanted to stay here. My house is like a jail compared to here."

I guess she's right, but I don't think of her house as a jail at all. It *is* cold-looking and gray, but it's still comfortable. But I know she's only saying that because she's sick of it. I wonder if I would be, too, if in her position.

"Would you like to come upstairs and see my room?" I ask awkwardly.

Emerson nods and follows me up the stairs. I feel like I'm acting weird, but I don't know how to *stop* acting weird. I try telling myself I know Emerson and we've spent time together before, but it just feels different now.

I open the door to my bedroom, which I cleaned for hours before this. I didn't want it to be messy and uncomfortable and, well, Emerson's rich. I didn't want her to judge me, even though I know in my brain she probably never would.

Even so, I borrowed cleaning supplies from Elise and Drew and cleaned this whole room so there isn't a speck of dust or a thing out of place. That's probably the only positive thing I've learned in foster care, really. Tons of foster parents have made me clean in the past. Now, I'm a pro.

I'm staring at my room proudly as Emerson takes it in. The polished-looking white walls, the gray carpet, freshly vacuumed. The full-sized bed pressed into the far left corner, with a plain white comforter and pillows that match. To me, this room is everything I've ever dreamed of.

But all she says is, "It's sad in here."

I look at her nervously. "Why do you say that?"

She notices my concerned face and relaxes hers. Reaching out to touch my arm, she explains, "I don't mean that in a bad way. I just mean you really need to make this room your own. You know, mess it up a little. Put things you like everywhere."

"I guess," I say, frowning. "I've never done that before. I've never been anywhere long enough, and I don't have my own money usually."

Emerson walks to my bed boldly and sits down, kicking off her battered shoes in the process. She lays on her stomach and looks at me casually, as if this isn't anything strange. "I'll help you. What kinds of things do you like?"

I sit next to her, crossing my legs underneath me. "Well, I don't know. I like music."

"Okay, that's definitely a start. You could collect CDs or vinyl or something. That would take up a lot of room and probably make you happy. In my room, I have a stack of all of Taylor Swift's magazines. I've been collecting them since I was ten."

I laugh because I'm amazed. "Really? That's awesome."

She gives me a proud smile. "Yeah, I take pride in that collection. And I always look at them, just because they make me happy. That's what you need. Things that put a smile on your face, even if you don't *need* them."

I can't help but think this is something she's learned from her parents, which isn't necessarily a bad thing, but I find it ironic since she seems to hate her parents. I wonder how it must feel to buy things for joy consistently. Are people who can do that always happy, or always unhappy? I can't figure out the answer, so I try and forget about it.

"I'll work on that," I tell Emerson, which makes her smile. "Do you wanna watch something?"

She nods, sitting up, and I get Kai's laptop. I open Netflix and we browse for a while before deciding on a show she's seen but I haven't. I haven't seen a lot of things, and I admit that to her, and she says we're going to have to catch me up on every single thing on Netflix. This seems like a great feat, but since it means I'll get to spend more time with Emerson, I don't mind it at all.

She persuades me to turn on the show merely by repeating, "It's the best show of all time!" over and over again until I *have* to watch it to actually understand why it's so good.

As the opening credits roll, Emerson asks, "You don't mind horror, right?"

"*Horror*?" I gasp. "We're watching a *horror* show?"

Emerson laughs and flops onto her stomach, getting comfortable with one of my pillows. "It's not *that* scary. And trust me, if you get frightened, I'll be here to comfort you." The sentiment is nice, but she says it with a snicker.

It isn't that I mind horror, it's just that it might be strange to watch something scary on a first date-thing. Or would it? I'm probably overthinking it, so I just lie down next to Emerson and settle in for whatever terror I'm about to witness.

I become engaged almost instantly. We don't do much talking, other than me asking if she wants a snack. We share the food Elise prepared and watch the screen. I wonder distantly if I should be doing more to entertain her, but it's hard to think when I am first of all invested in this film, and second of all touching shoulders with her.

About halfway through the movie, I notice she's looking at me out of the corner of her eye. Laughing nervously, I meet her eyes. Did she say something I missed? I've been so focused on the movie I suppose she could've said a monologue and I wouldn't have noticed.

But she doesn't say anything in response to my nervousness, just keeps looking. She swallows hard and puts her attention to the laptop finally.

"Is everything okay?" I ask softly.

I watch Emerson breathe in deeply. Her eyes trace my face once more in a way that seems very intimate, and those butterflies in my stomach take flight. "Remember when I gave you my number because I said you had a crush on me?"

I nod my head, feeling my heart flutter.

"I never knew if you did," she admits. "It was because I had a crush on *you*."

I bite the inside of my cheek, feeling my cheeks grow hot. "You did? Or you do?"

But she doesn't reply. I notice her eyes flit to my lips briefly before she's moving closer to me, and my mind goes completely blank. I can't think of *anything*. I always thought I'd be remembering every romantic comedy I'd ever seen, remembering how to do this, remembering to do *something*, but all I see is white as Emerson presses her lips to mine.

And I can't stop thinking I'm dreaming. It's all I *can* think of, other than the warmth and softness of her lips I've looked at so many times. Other than the salty taste of popcorn on her mouth and the feeling of her hand touching my face. The way I feel her breath against my cheek and hair against my hand as I—

A loud knock on the door scares us apart.

We stare at each other breathlessly, both of our cheeks flushed, and look at my bedroom door. But the knock hadn't been on my door, and we realize it at the same time, when we heard a commotion from downstairs in the foyer.

I hear Elise's voice first, asking someone what they're doing here, and then a man's voice. It could be Drew's, but I'm not completely sure.

"What's going on?" Emerson asks, but I shake my head because I don't know.

We sit completely silently, waiting to hear more noise, but there's nothing but low talking. Elise calls for me to come downstairs. For some reason, it terrifies me. Between the fact Elise and Drew have not been acting right and the fact this seems unexpected, I can somehow tell this is not going to be good.

"Will you come with me?" I ask Emerson shakily. I feel my hands form into fists, clenching and unclenching slowly. She nods and follows me out of the room.

The pair of us walk downstairs quickly, but my steps slow when I see who's here. A jarring cold spreads from my chest outward, my skin paling, any hope I had drying up completely.

"What are you doing here?" I ask blankly. My mouth feels like it's full of cotton, my head of light air that threatens to make me faint. Coherent thoughts leave my brain as I take in the gelled-back, dull brown hair, the stony black eyes, the jaw that's been set since birth with perpetual distaste.

"It's time to go, Lavender," Jacob says. his voice pushy and dominating. "Go upstairs and gather your things.

CHAPTER SEVENTEEN

"What are you talking about?" I demand. As I look around slowly, I take in all of the Kahales and their faces and the way they look devastated. We all stand around Jacob in a way that shows he's clearly in charge of something here.

My gaze lands on Elise first. The expression on her face is angry, something that isn't typical of her. Her arms are crossed over her chest defensively, while she stares at Jacob's stony face, but when she looks at me, she looks like she could melt with sadness. Drew looks similar. He stands behind his wife, a protective hand on her shoulder. He reminds me of a wilted flower, posture drooping, frown bringing out deep wrinkles around his mouth.

And there's Leia and Kai. Leia's lip quivers, her hands bunched up in fists so hard they shake. I don't know what she knows, what Jacob has already said, what her parents have already told her, but it seems like this is as much a surprise to her as it is to me. She refuses to meet my eyes but instead locks onto the floor, sniffing loudly. Kai doesn't give me much. Maybe he's hiding whatever he's feeling or doesn't know how to feel yet. Or perhaps he just doesn't care.

I take all of this in and still feel paranoia pounding on my brain, demanding attention. I know if I were to let myself, I could believe this was a setup. I could believe this was on purpose.

"Lavender, I—" Elise tries to say, her voice steady, but Jacob interrupts her.

"We need to leave. I'm sorry, Lavender, but you knew what would happen if this placement didn't work out." His voice is devoid of emotion, purely business. The angry lilt to his voice tells me he's losing his patience.

I narrow my eyes. "So this *isn't* working out? According to who?"

He looks at Elise as if waiting for her response, and though my stomach drops, I nod coldly. "Oh. Got it."

With my arms crossed across my chest, I wait for anyone to speak up and tell me it isn't true, the Kahales *aren't* kicking me out right now. Not only that, but they didn't even tell me. *They didn't even prepare me.*

"Lavender, you are clearly not doing well here," Jacob explains, like he cares, which I know he doesn't. His hands are tucked tightly in his jean pockets, jaw tightening as he continues. "Elise called me and told me about the night you ran away, and I've spent a lot of time finding a really good group home for you to go to. But it's time to go now—"

"No, that *isn't* how it happened Jacob, I just—" Elise attempts to explain herself again, stepping forward, but Jacob continues as if she hasn't spoken.

"—and you'll be moving to the group home as soon as they have a spot open for you in a few weeks." The look he gives Elise is pointed, sharp, and somewhere deep inside of me I feel a swelling protectiveness that screams, *He can't look at her like that.* I swallow it down, the lump in my throat aching.

I feel tears filling my eyes, but it isn't sadness that fills my veins. Instead, it's fire. My nails dig into my arms and my skin grows hot and red. I'm ashamed I didn't see this coming, that I feel betrayed. I try to keep my breathing controlled, in and out slowly, but the blood rushing to my ears just makes me feel like I'm huffing and puffing and making a scene.

"I tried getting you into the group home sooner, it just didn't work out. So I've found a temporary place that will hopefully be better for you," Jacob says. Now, his broad arms are crossed, too. He looks annoyed at having to explain himself.

"*Nowhere* is better than here," I spit. Then I look Elise in the face and say, "Or, that's what I thought, at least."

She looks simply horrified at the prospect that this *wouldn't* be the best place for me, but how could I not doubt? How could I *not* be filled with sheer anger and paranoia when the one family I was learning to trust may have betrayed me in the most detrimental way possible?

"You were right, Lavender," Elise says softly, walking closer to me. But my guard is up. It hurts that I can feel my view of her altering no matter how focused I'm trying to keep my mind. Is Elise capable of sending me off like this with no remorse? My brain is torn. "This *is* where you belong, but I didn't know what to do that night. We've been trying to get you out of this, I—"

"But you didn't even tell me!" I reiterate. I wipe away a tear that escaped, feeling the warmth in my eyes that threatens more. Now is not the time to cry, though. I'm embarrassed for being so heartbroken. "How could you? How could you pretend like everything was fine when really I was going to be kicked out?"

"You aren't being kicked out," she insists, her hands pleading. "We want you more than anything. It was a mistake I didn't tell you, I'm sorry, I'm so sorry, I thought if I talked to CPS we could get you to stay, but—"

"But it's time to go," Jacob interjects. Everyone's eyes land on him, on the hard set to his jaw, the way his brow is tensed. I wonder if he can feel how unwelcome he is here.

"Lavender, what's going on?" a small voice says from behind me, and it's at this moment I realize Emerson is still here.

I turn around and she pales a bit when she sees my face.

"I'm leaving. That's what's going on," I say emptily. The pain that blossoms in my chest at hearing it out loud is almost debilitating.

Elise finally steps forward, her eyes glossy as well. In fact, the entire Kahale family looks like they're fighting back tears. My brain continues its battle. Is it a ruse? Is it sincerity?

"I never intended for this to happen, Lavender, you have to understand," Elise pleads.

"I don't know that I can, Elise. How can I trust you?" My voice breaks and I look at my shoes.

"This is entirely a misunderstanding!" Drew chimes in, approaching Jacob. "We can work something out. But Lavender belongs with us."

Quite rudely, Jacob explains, "Unfortunately, misunderstanding or not, I have to take her out of here tonight. People have been contacted and a bed has been prepared. Take it up with CPS another time. Right now it's time for Lavender to leave."

"You can't take her," Elise says to Jacob stonily. "You can't. She isn't prepared for this. We hadn't even spoken to her, Jacob, it can't happen like this."

"I'm sorry, Elise," Jacob says with a shrug. "Like I said, we can revisit this. Just not tonight."

"No," Emerson suddenly says firmly. My heart catches at her interference, and I grab her hand absentmindedly.

She squeezes tight, her palm sweaty. "You can't just take her out of her *home*. This is where Lavender should be, not in a group home."

Jacob looks at Emerson with confusion since he doesn't know her. "This technically *isn't* Lavender's home. Right now we just need to find the place where she can do best in, and since she felt like she had to run away, it clearly isn't here."

Emerson walks past me, and I don't stop her because I know whatever she's going to say won't help. And maybe it'll make her feel better to feel like she tried, like she was involved, even if this is futile. "But she made a mistake! It was just one mistake and she fixed it because she came right back home! There has to be something you can do."

But Jacob just shakes his head, staring down at Emerson with ice coating his features. He doesn't care about emotions. He cares about his job. "I'm sorry, but there isn't. The arrangements have already been made."

"*Bullshit*!" she exclaims, making everyone including me jump. "You can't take her away! Look, sir, my dad's rich, and I'm sure he could give you *any* amount of money you—"

"Emerson!" I cry, grasping her arm. I'm shocked at her behavior and fighting for me. I'll admit, some part of me wishes Emerson could drop tons of money for me, but the other part knows that's ridiculous and unethical. I don't need money. I'm past that kind of help. "There's nothing you can do."

When Emerson faces me she's crying, and the ache in my chest spreads until I feel like a walking bruise. I never expected her to cry for me, to ever even care if I left. It feels strange having people who might want me around. Strange and hurtful and bittersweet. "There has to be something. You can't leave. I'm only just starting to know you."

"I have no choice, apparently." My voice is empty. "I wouldn't have chosen this. But I'm not in control of my own life like you're in control of yours. I have to leave."

My throat aches as the words come out of my mouth, and Emerson looks shattered. I don't completely understand why, but I understand her feelings. I understand how important consistency is and how difficult this is, not only for her.

Before I let myself sob or punch something or fall to the floor, though, I run upstairs and start packing, shoving all my old things away like I'm used to doing. Stumbling upon my lavender blanket sends my head spinning, and I'm about to take it, about to put it into the bag, but something stops me. Instead, I fold it nicely on the bed that was once mine and don't look back at it once.

* * *

I'm in the same car I came to the Kahales in. I feel like I'm going to be sick. I am freezing to the bone and no amount of heat could cure this chill. It runs deeper than temperature. I don't know if I'll ever feel warm again.

I had to run out of the Kahales' house so I wouldn't think twice about it. I forced the tears away and went on autopilot, stuffing my meager pile of belongings into my torn backpack, filling my brain with TV static so my thoughts wouldn't spiral. While I did, the Kahales fought with Jacob the entire time. I heard their voices, raised and tearful, and even with that, it's hard for me to really know what happened and how I feel about it. Because what if they decided to let me go before we got close? Why didn't they call it off or at the very least talk to me about it?

Emerson came up to my room with me and tried to help me pack but I ignored her because I knew I would fall to my knees if I spoke one more word. It was the type of sad that simmered below the surface but would bubble over at the simplest, *Are you okay?*

When I actually left, walked out the door, everyone was saying goodbye and asking me to wait, but I couldn't. I didn't. I just walked away.

I got into the car and stared at the floor until we were well out of Springfield so I didn't explode all over Jacob's car, which today smells like gasoline and cigarettes. It's horrific.

We've been driving for half an hour already. Jacob has tried saying useless things to me I have completely ignored because I'd rather jump out of this moving car than say one word to him. I know he's doing his job, but it is extremely hard to remind myself of this when I remember he's ruined my final chance at a forever home, which just happened to be the best home in all of America. Now, that's gone. It's over.

There's no going back there, and I don't think I have fully processed this yet. Some part of me believes later tonight I'll be watching a movie with the Kahales while eating salty popcorn and laughing at nonsense. But there's no way I could ever go back.

The hushed conversations between Elise and Drew are beginning to make sense now. I feel bad for Leia and Kai if they really didn't know about this. Especially for Leia, I know she isn't a huge fan of sudden changes. But for them both, I know they aren't used to having secrets with their parents. I know this isn't something they're used to.

Thinking of this reminds me of the last look Leia gave me. It shot daggers into my heart, watching her cry and try to keep composure while she waved at me. I could've broken down, screamed, sobbed, and banged my fists on the ground right then and there.

Perhaps I'm conceited, but some part of me is surprised Kai and Leia didn't fight for me. Were they scared? Were they told not to say anything? Did they just not care?

I don't think I'll ever have closure on any part of my life at the Kahales, but what hurts the most is I will never know what could've happened between me and Emerson. I think back to a little over an hour ago, when we were sitting upon my bed and kissing. My first kiss.

And now my life is ruined. Everything is in shambles. Maybe I won't ever kiss someone again, and that was it, and it wasn't even complete.

Jacob turns into the driveway of a ranch-style house that has no outdoor lights. Only light coming from the smallest window I've ever seen. It doesn't even tell me there's a house there. Once again, the sick feeling returns, and I have to force air into my lungs.

We get out of the car, and I slam the door shut. Jacob tells me to relax, and I glare at him as hard as possible. He leads me up to the front door and knocks, the sound seeming to echo down the silent street. In the distance, I hear a dog barking, and it smells like dirt where we stand.

It takes a minute, but the door eventually opens and a short, plump old woman pops her head out. Her gray hair is tied back and her face is covered in wrinkles. The smell of cigarette smoke oozes out of the doorway and I stifle a gag.

"Welcome," she says simply, her voice gravelly. She doesn't sound overly mean, but I don't suspect she'll be my new mom anytime soon.

"Thank you for this, Elizabeth. I really appreciate it," Jacob says to the woman, who nods and mutters how it's no problem.

"I'd like to be shown to my room now," I say miserably. I'm losing my composure, and I know it's a matter of seconds before the dam breaks.

Elizabeth looks at me with a sour face, mutters, "*No manners,*" and moves aside so I can come in. Jacob doesn't stay; he says goodbye to Elizabeth and walks back to his car. Elizabeth walks me down the hallway and gestures to a room painted green to the left, and I walk in without question, slamming the door in her face.

I throw my things down on the floor and jump on the first bed I see, which is covered in a yellowish quilt that looks a million years old. When I land on it, I swear I taste dust billowing around me.

But I don't allow myself to care right now. Instead, I allow myself to feel this terrible hurt. This terrible betrayal I've avoided feeling until right now. And before I can stop myself, I'm sobbing into the discolored pillow beneath me to muffle the sound.

I give myself a couple of minutes to cry. And then Emerson's face is floating into my brain, followed by the breathing exercise she did with me that first night. Without opening my eyes, so I can focus on Emerson's face, I breathe deeply as if we're doing it together.

I open my eyes when my breathing is controlled, when I feel better after letting it out. Through the haze of tears, my eyes focus on a little girl sitting on the bed on the other side of the room.

I flinch, surprised by her presence, but the expression on her young face is calm and curious. She swings her legs back and forth leisurely. She's small, maybe around seven or eight. She wears purple glasses that make her dark brown eyes look too big, and her skin is a warm, dark brown.

"Get out!" I shout immediately.

Her face contorts angrily as she snaps back, "No, you! This is *my* room!"

I look to the ceiling, praying to whoever's up there and notice brown stains, which makes me look away immediately. "Oh, you've got to be kidding me. I'm not sharing this room with you."

Her eyes narrowed, she crosses her arms across her chest in a way that reminds me painfully of myself. "Oh. yes, you are. Elizabeth said so. I hope you're nice."

Covering my face with my hands, I shake my head miserably, wondering what I did to deserve this. Paradise, paradise for *weeks*, and now this dungeon with a tiny ball of sass.

"Who are you?" she asks me.

I look up at the stains again, sighing loudly. "Lavender. Who are you?"

"Sadie. And that's Oscar," she says, pointing at a spot on the dull wood floor. For the first time, I notice a little boy who looks identical to Sadie. The only difference is he's sitting with his knees pulled up under his chin, his eyes closed as if he's asleep.

"Jeez! How are you two so quiet?"

Sadie shrugs, swinging her legs once more. "My momma calls us kittens. She says she has to put a bell on us to know we're there."

Despite myself, I smile. I wonder where their mother is, but I'm too afraid to ask.

"Are you twins?" I ask.

Sadie nods, glancing over at her brother. "I'm older by three minutes. My momma said I had to come into the world first because my brother can't live without me."

I feel a tremor of sadness run through me at that, but don't let it show. I've met tons of other foster kids in situations like this. But it never makes it any easier to see we're all screwed up in one way or another.

"And how old are you?"

She returns her glare to me, and it's pretty angry for such a young kid. "Eight. What about *you*, crybaby?"

I try hard not to let my amusement show. "Sixteen."

Her eyebrows shoot up. "Wow. That's old."

"I guess it is."

"Do you know your momma?"

I shake my head and focus on the wall in front of me instead of Sadie's face. "Nope. Never did. Not my dad, either."

"Yeah, I don't know my dad. My momma said we were too good for him."

"I think your mom's probably right. She sounds really smart."

Sadie smiles big, revealing one missing tooth. "She is. She's coming to get us next week."

"Oh, yeah?"

She nods proudly. "She said she's getting better for us. Oscar and me. And she's better now. I just know it."

I give her an encouraging smile, and I hope she doesn't notice how fake it is. I hope she's right about her mom, because, from the sounds of it, she might not be in the right mindset to take care of two children right now. I obviously don't know the whole situation, but it still worries me.

"She really is," Sadie insists, getting defensive. "A lot of bad stuff happened to my mom, Oscar, and me, but it's gonna be better now. I just know it."

"Okay. I believe you."

Sadie looks satisfied as she leans back against her pillows, looking at her brother with a caring expression on her face.

"Oscar doesn't talk anymore," she says suddenly.

"He doesn't, huh?"

Sadie shakes her head, and her face turns sad. "We saw someone get hurt. It was a man with my mom and they had something the police officers wanted, but Momma and the man didn't want to give it to them, and they had guns."

My stomach churns as she talks. I wonder if Sadie has much company other than Elizabeth or if she's been here a while all by herself, with the exception of Oscar, who obviously doesn't engage in many conversations.

"I'm really sorry, Sadie." And I am. I feel shitty sitting here and feeling bad for myself when Oscar and Sadie have been through a great deal already, and they're only eight.

"It's okay." Sadie shrugs, eyes still on her brother. "I like being with Oscar. But he used to tell really funny jokes sometimes. Do you know how to make him say something?"

I can't decide if she's genuinely asking me or preparing to show me, so I uncertainly reply with a no.

Sadie's face grows grim. She looks far too old, and it's terrifying to see. "Me either. But Momma always says be patient, so that's what I'll do."

"I think that's a good idea. You guys will be okay."

We don't say anything after that. As silence fills the room, I'm left to my own thoughts. But my brain is so shocked by the events of tonight it suppresses them, focusing on Sadie and Oscar, whose situation is right in front of my face at the moment. I make a conscious—but hardly healthy—decision to focus on them while I'm here. I can't deal with the hurt right now. And once I'm at the group home, I will be at my final destination. No more homes. Then I'll think this through. Then I'll allow myself to feel.

After a while, I realize Sadie's fallen asleep. Oscar is curled up right next to her bed, and I consider putting a blanket over him, but I don't want to do something he's uncomfortable with and risk overstimulating him. So I leave him be and stare at the ceiling until sleep claims me.

* * *

I wake before the sun, feeling like I never fell asleep. My eyes are puffy, my head aches, and my throat bone dry. I sit up in the lumpy bed, looking around the room as the memories come back to me. It's hard to remember they're real, and I find myself trying to focus on my surroundings. The walls were obviously white once, but now they're yellowed. The smell of cigarette smoke is heavy in here, and I assume that's why the walls have turned that nasty shade. In the dark, I can just make out Sadie's bed diagonally from me, the twin to the bed in which I currently sit. The room is sad. So dull and sad it makes me sigh. I'm not with the Kalahes anymore, that's for certain. I'm here with Sadie and Oscar who, obviously, have already become my problem.

I sit still for as long as I physically can before being driven to the bathroom by my full bladder. It takes a few minutes to find it in the dark, but it's a small house, so I find it eventually.

After that, I risk heading to the kitchen, which I know I saw when I first came into the house. The lights are off in there too, but I find the sink and drink straight from the tap. I don't want to explore the fridge to find out if it's locked or anything yet, so I know this is my best bet right now.

When I turn around, I flinch.

Oscar sits silently on the living room couch, beside one single table lamp, using its glow to read a chapter book. I hadn't even noticed he'd gotten up.

I make my way to the couch and sit beside him. I know he won't speak, but I find myself greeting him anyways.

"Hey, Oscar, what's up?" I look at his book to see if I recognize it, but I don't. "What are you reading?"

Of course, he doesn't reply, just keeps on reading. He has glasses just like Sadie, but they're dark blue. He wears a matching blue pajama set and blue socks, so I begin to wonder if his favorite color is blue.

"You like blue, huh?" I ask. And even though there will never be an answer, I feel like I want to keep talking. "I like blue, too. Although I might like purple better. I like lavender things, I'd say. Some people think it's cheesy to like things from your name, like Summer or April, but I love lavender things. It's probably the only thing I have from my mom, you know? And even though I hate that she left me, she's still a part of me, I guess, and I—"

"What are you doing?"

I look up to see Sadie standing in the hallway, her hair messy atop her head. She looks at me with pure confusion.

"Why are you talking to my brother?" she asks again, putting her hands on her hips. "No one talks to him except for me."

"Okay. I'm sorry."

She looks shocked by my compliance. I'm sure that doesn't typically go over well with others.

"You should be," she tells me, looking proud and defiant. Turning to Oscar, she says, "Oscar, you have to get dressed before Elizabeth wakes up."

Oscar closes his book and stands, walks to Sadie and takes her hand.

But before they walk away, Sadie says, "We clean on Saturdays. The cleaning stuff is in the closet at the end of the hall."

I sigh loudly. No, this *definitely* isn't the Kahales. But I got what I wanted at the beginning, didn't I? The same old foster home I've been in from the moment I entered the system.

How will I ever forgive the Kahales for this?

CHAPTER EIGHTEEN

To my dismay, Sadie tells me the whole house needs to be clean by noon. She tells me I'm lucky I got up early without knowing, because Elizabeth wouldn't like it if I slept in. As Sadie and I clean, we talk about a lot of things.

She starts by telling me about Elizabeth and how she isn't the worst person ever, but she certainly isn't the best, either. Since she's old, she can't do a lot of the cleaning, so she makes us kids do it. Though Elizabeth has never harshly punished Sadie or Oscar, she gets very unhappy and often makes them go to bed without dinner if they misbehave.

I find this pretty standard, but Sadie hasn't been in as many foster homes as me, obviously. She tells me this is her third and the first time she was in the system, she went because of what happened with her mom and the man, who I assume may have been her mom's boyfriend or something to that effect. That was when Sadie and Oscar went to two homes, and they were readmitted into the system when their mom started using drugs more often. They've been here at Elizabeth's for almost a year, Sadie says, and they haven't been moved because it's been working out okay for everyone involved.

But Sadie is convinced her mother will be coming to pick her up this week, which is one of the reasons why I was allowed to come here. Elizabeth doesn't really have the room for a lot of kids here and typically wouldn't like more than two.

Sadie talks about how her mother is in what I assume is rehab and how she's excited to see her mom again. My heart aches for her and Oscar but I try not to let it show I have doubts about their mother coming through. Instead, I ask Sadie about what her and her mom will do when she gets picked up. This sends Sadie on an hour-long rant about all the lovely things they'll do, and by the end of it, I'm wishing I didn't ask. I can tell Sadie is counting on this, and I hope for her sake her mom has really pulled it together.

Elizabeth comes out of her bedroom at almost exactly noon. She gives us an approving nod when she sees the cleaning we've done and goes right to the kitchen, where she starts cooking breakfast for the three of us. I'm sure it will be nothing compared to the Kahales' pancakes, but it will have to do.

Us three kids and Elizabeth sit at the round kitchen table when the food's all done. I find it awkward we all sit together because of the dysfunctionality of it all. Elizabeth doesn't consider us family—why would she?—but also makes sure we're all sitting together for dinner, as if that will erase years of feeling left out of family meals. But Oscar and Sadie are used to this, used to feeling a little weird sitting at someone else's dinner table. They pig out on Elizabeth's runny eggs and soggy bacon until they're full. Meanwhile, I try to get as much of it down as possible, but by the end, I'm feeling a little nauseous. I've been too spoiled for the past couple of weeks.

When we're all finished, Elizabeth asks Sadie to take all the dishes to the sink, to which Sadie replies with a loud sigh.

"It's Lavender's turn, she just got here!" she exclaims, frustrated.

"Oh, I can do it," I say casually, if only because I don't want there to be a conflict. I can't say I even mind doing dishes, anyway.

But Elizabeth gives me a stern look. "No, Sadie will do it. It's her turn."

"When's it *your* turn, you lazy old bag?" Sadie snaps.

I'd laugh if it weren't such a telling moment.

Before Elizabeth can say a word, I gesture for Sadie to calm down. "Sadie, don't say that. I'll help you bring up the dishes, let's go."

Both of us go to the sink. Elizabeth leaves the room, and Oscar rests his head against the table like he's listening to the wood. His eyes are on his sister adoringly, though.

While we're rinsing the plates, I say to Sadie gently, "You should try to be more respectful."

She looks at me in surprise. "What do *you* care? Don't you hate them as much as me?"

I chuckle lightly. "It's not *them* you're supposed to hate. It's the system that puts us here, not them. Just try to keep quiet when you feel angry, is all I'm saying. It'll get you farther than speaking out in our world."

Sadie rolls her eyes, reminding me of myself again. I bite the inside of my cheek hard. Sadie says, "Whatever. My mom's getting me on Monday, anyway."

I don't reply because I don't want to hear about her mother anymore. I don't want to hear her little naive hopes for the future because I know exactly how it feels when each one is squashed. She has too much of what I had at her age, and it terrifies me. No wonder I am who I am. I didn't listen to the advice I gave to Sadie and earned myself a *reputation*.

All I can think is how I can't let that happen to her. I'd be failing myself if I did.

So for the rest of the day, I try to tell Sadie all of the things I wish I knew when I was eight. Starting, of course, with being respectful to foster parents *unless* they are exhibiting abusive behaviors. In which case, yeah—fight like hell to get out.

"But sometimes foster parents are mean to my brother," she explains firmly, her eyebrows raised, "and that is *not* okay."

"I agree," I say as I wash the sink. "So fight for him and for yourself when you feel threatened. But there's no reason to say anything disrespectful if there isn't a reason. Got it?"

And for the whole day, Sadie says she gets it, but it doesn't even matter because she'll be out of here soon enough. And every time she does, my heart hurts. I agree with her every time, say "just in case," and move on to the next thing.

As we're working on lunch, chopping up vegetables for a salad, I tell her, "Don't be rude to your social workers, either. Actually, say nothing to them besides yes or no. They hate that. So you're being rude without *really* being rude."

Sadie laughs at that, dumping red peppers into a wide glass bowl.

"They can't say you've done anything if you haven't, Sadie. You have to stay out of trouble."

She sighs, clearly done with my lecturing. "I get it! I have to be good!"

More time passes, and we're working on making a pot of coffee for Elizabeth so she can have some after dinner. I get to the most important piece of advice I could ever give, so I stop what I'm doing and make sure Sadie is paying attention.

"The *number one* thing I have to tell you is *never*, and I mean *never*, run away. Did you get that?"

"I got that," she repeats dismissively. I can tell she probably *doesn't* "got that" because of the bored look in her eyes. But it quickly changes to interest as she looks at me and asks, "Did you ever run away?"

"Yes," I say, looking away uncomfortably. I'd never plant my own bad decisions into an impressionable young mind, especially one like Sadie's. I know she'd take it, digest it, and reserve it for the future. I would've done the same at her age. "But it wasn't worth it. It never is."

Two hours later, Sadie and I are crashing into our beds, sighing deeply. It's been a long day, and even though the bed is lumpy and smells like mildew, it feels good to rest.

I lay listening to Sadie speaking softly to Oscar across the room for a little while, until I hear my phone vibrating from under my bed. I reach for it and notice a text from Emerson to my surprise.

It reads: *Where are you? What happened? Is everything okay?*

I reply: *I'm fine. I'm at a new foster home.*

What's the address? I'll drive there tonight.

I sigh as I type back. *I'm sorry, but I can't tell you that. There are other kids here.*

She doesn't respond for a few moments, and I think I might be off the hook. But then my phone starts ringing.

"Hello?" I say.

"You have to run away," she says without precedent.

"Excuse me?"

I hear fumbling on her end as if she's moving around a lot. "You can't stay there. You belong here. I'll come get you."

I scoff. "Emerson, I can't just run away. You know I can't just run away."

Emerson sniffles, which is alarming. "I don't think I can do this without you, Lavender. I've never had someone like you in my life, and I don't know how to just forget about it."

I take a deep breath and shut my eyes, feeling the pressure of her words sink into me. "Emerson—"

"I let so many trivial things prevent us from being closer and I regret it so much. I can't believe I cared what anyone else thought." At this point, I can tell she's full-on crying, and I'm caught between confusion and heartbreak. "It's so soon, I know, but I can't help but think this was the beginning of something."

"What?" My mind reels with her admittance and I wonder if I'd felt the same, if I thought Emerson and I were a beginning. I guess I did, but some part of me was always sure nothing would ever be permanent, even after I actually *wanted* to be at the Kahales. I'd still had my defenses up just in case, and as it turned out, my intuition actually led me to the right place for once.

"I'm serious, Lavender. I need you to come back." Her voice is pleading and serious, more serious than I've ever heard it before. Distantly I wonder why this hadn't been said before. Not enough time? Or maybe she just realized this.

Probably, my paranoia chimes in, *she doesn't mean it.*

I swallow hard, forcing away the lump in my throat that forms with the frustration and confusion of it all. "I'm sorry," I say, and thankfully my voice is steady, "but I can't leave. I can't just do that. It wouldn't be safe for me."

She won't take that as an answer, though, and her voice raises. "I'll *make* it safe! Please. You promised you weren't gonna leave."

But I'm growing tired and annoyed. I know what I said that night under the stars. That I wasn't going anywhere and I would be there. But I was naïve. Things like *staying* aren't things I can promise. And as horrible as I feel about it, I can't let her suck me back into a life that very obviously isn't mine.

"Emerson, the Kahales made their decision when they let me go. I'm not theirs. It was just another stop for me. And right now I have to make my own decision for my own safety. The Kahales are behind me. Springfield is behind me. And you have to be, too. Goodbye, Emerson."

CHAPTER NINETEEN

"Today's the day! Today's the day!"

I jolt awake to the feeling of someone jumping on me and go on high alert, immediately seeing Sadie's huge eyes hovering above me.

"Huh? What's today?" I say, acting like I don't know.

"Momma's coming today!" she exclaims, her smile taking up half her face.

"No kidding, Sadie. Now get off me!" I shout playfully.

She climbs down from my bed and I sit up, rubbing the sleep out of my eyes. As I yawn, I notice all of Sadie's things are packed up and her bed is made. It's Monday morning and, you guessed it, Sadie and Oscar could potentially be going home with their mom today.

I should be at school, theoretically, but I won't be starting at the new one until Wednesday since my paperwork didn't get processed over the weekend. I'm fine with it, but I could tell Elizabeth wasn't thrilled when she got that call from Jacob yesterday. Even though it's clear she relies on us to do her housework for her, the way she grumbles under her breath when she enters the same room as one of us tells me she misses her alone time.

"You all ready to go, kiddo?" I ask, gesturing to her empty side of the room.

"Yep! And I packed up Oscar's room, too," she announces proudly. Her smile is excited and steady. The sight of it makes my cheeks ache.

I nod and smile, hoping I don't have to put up the pretense of feeling excited for her and Oscar for much longer. A selfish—but practical—part of me hopes their mom doesn't come today. Who knows if she's actually in the mental state to take care of them? If she is, by all means, she should take them. But maybe it would be beneficial for everyone involved if these two were in the system for just a bit longer.

I sound like a hypocrite, but I guess I'm beginning to understand why adults are the way they are after spending a lot of time with Sadie and hearing her story and struggles. It's hard to get through to someone who's been through a trauma. I know because I'm someone who's been through trauma, and I often find myself too scared to let anyone in. It's embarrassing for me to even admit. Of course, some adults simply don't care about children and want to make them obedient, but not everyone is like that. So perhaps I understand the tough love now. Perhaps I understand some people in my life weren't trying to hurt me, they were trying to help me in the ways they knew how, the ways they thought were best for me.

I get out of bed with a pit in my stomach, worry gnawing at my brain for these kids. I busy myself with making myself presentable for the day before making my bed and straightening up the meager items I have. It's the usual stuff: the stolen book, the ripped pairs of jeans, and wrinkled notebooks. The only difference now is I have a new sweatshirt, one I didn't even mean to take with me. When I see it, I shove it to the bottom of my bag and refuse to look at it again. Afterward, Elizabeth calls us to the living room to help her with something on the television.

Through it all, Sadie talks our ears off, which she also did yesterday. Sadie can be sassy and mature when she wants, but she's still just a kid, and it shows. I'm glad she's still a kid, but I'm terrified of what could happen if her hopes crash tonight.

Elizabeth doesn't even tell Sadie to stop talking today, to lower her voice. She did that tons yesterday. But after Elizabeth and I share a look, I know she has the same concerns I do. I wonder if she might even know something we don't yet.

We continue with our day doing basically nothing except what Elizabeth finds for us to do. She isn't used to having kids home during the day, so I'm sure she's not as into it as we are. At some point, she asks if we can prepare lunch and dinner and she'll help us cook it when it's time. Sadie's so jittery she says yes, and I'm so bored I give in.

We prepare a simple lunch of bologna sandwiches and iced tea. When we're finished, we all eat, except for Oscar who seems to hate the bologna on the sandwich. Sadie busies herself with removing the meat, and Oscar proceeds to eat the white bread slowly.

When we're finished with that, we're all still bored. Sadie is shaking her leg so fast the table shakes. I wish I had more to say to her, but I don't. Or, I have *tons* to say, words that would never stop flowing if I had the chance, but I know I can't. I know saying anything would be tricky. The soft part of me that formed so quickly over the past couple of weeks just wants to start begging and pleading and getting back to the way things were. I'd grown so accustomed to change because of my time in the system, and this is my first time ever really missing a place. Ever missing people. And I hate to say it, but I can't help but think about what I'd be doing right now if I were at the Kahales. Or what the Kahales are doing right now.

Kai's probably in his last period of school. Yeah, that's right. I think it might be math for him. I'd be in art. *With Emerson.*

I shut my eyes at the thought of her and take deep breaths until I stop smelling her scent in the air: citrus and expensive perfume and sometimes watermelon because she chewed watermelon gum in school. And thinking about her popping a stick of pink gum in her mouth, walking through fluorescent-lit hallways, still looking like a model on a runway, makes me think about the feeling of her lips on mine. The taste of salt on her lips. The pounding in my chest, followed by the shattering of my heart when I told her I had to let her go.

I am stuck in time as the minutes go by. Somewhere miles away from where I am, Sadie complains. A lot.

"What time is it now?" she asks impatiently.

I'm forced to respond when no one else budges. "Four-oh-three," I say.

"It was four-oh-two ten minutes ago!"

I laugh. "Sure feels like it, doesn't it?"

She plops down on the couch hard, a scowl on her face. She crosses her arms tightly across her chest. "This was supposed to be the best day ever. Where is she?"

"I don't know," I say with a shrug. "Maybe they hit traffic."

"Traffic?" she asks suspiciously. "I don't know about that."

"Well… maybe they stopped for dinner," I suggest, bordering annoyance. I want to go back to thinking about Emerson and her pestering isn't helping.

Sadie looks at me like I'm an idiot. "At four?"

I sigh, exasperated. "I don't know! Just trying to help."

But I know I'm not helping, so I decide to shut up and let her pace around. We're long past telling her to stop. This kid is anxious, and I don't blame her. I'm growing more anxious as the time passes, if only just because *she* is, too.

"Come on, Sadie. Go get Oscar from the bedroom and we'll start on dinner," I suggest.

She hesitates but decides it's for the best and heads down the hall to get Oscar. When they both come into the room, Oscar has his nose stuck in his book and has to be led to the table by Sadie so he doesn't bang into something. Oscar doesn't really like to help us with cooking or cleaning, but he does like to be a part of it. At one point yesterday, I started washing the dishes before him and Sadie came back in the room, and he actually turned his nose up at me.

While Sadie takes the frozen vegetables out of the freezer, I begin reading the back of the package of instant mashed potatoes Elizabeth set out for us to make. A silence settles upon the kitchen as we're all focusing, but it is interrupted by a sudden knock at the door.

Sadie gasps, dropping a bag of frozen peas. She runs to the door and it's open in an instant, an icy gust of wind blowing into the house along with a few snowflakes. My heart clenches at the sight, mostly because being here has made me feel so disconnected from the outside world, I didn't even know it was snowing outside.

I go after her, but stop when I see Sadie's facial expression as she stares up at someone at the door. Her face has fallen from excitement to dread, and her small hand slips off the doorknob numbly. Elizabeth has risen from her chair in the living room, and even *her* face has fallen from its usual grimace.

"What is it, Sadie?" I ask nervously, coming to the door.

Standing in the doorway is a tall white man, who is clearly not her mother.

"What are you doing here, Gabriel? Is Momma in the car?" Sadie asks hesitantly, her eyes wide and scared.

I'd assume this is her social worker, but I've never seen him before. I watch as he shakes his head sadly, looking at the ground.

"But where *is* she?" Sadie demands.

Gabriel gets down to her height and looks her in the eyes when he says, "I'm sorry, Sadie, but your mother isn't ready for you just yet. She's still not better. But we've found a better, more permanent foster home for you and your brother for now, and we'll keep you in contact with your mother. How does that sound?"

"No!" she spits. "That's what you said last time! I want to see her *now*!"

But Gabriel shakes his head, at a loss for words. He's more sympathetic than Jacob, at least, but this is still hard for a kid. I don't blame Sadie for being upset.

I look behind me when I hear sniffling and see Oscar is on the verge of tears at seeing and hearing all of this. I am caught between wanting to comfort him and wanting to be there for Sadie.

"It's time for you to get your things," Gabriel says finally.

"Go on, Sadie, you—" Elizabeth says calmly, attempting at keeping control, but Sadie isn't interested.

She balls her hands into fists, shouting, "I hate you!" directly at Gabriel, who looks defeated.

She turns and runs down the hall into the bedroom, and I follow her immediately. She is sat on my bed, of all places, and seems to be holding her breath. When I approach her, she sucks in a bunch of air and holds it, her chest puffed out.

"Sadie?" I say gently, sitting down next to her.

She lets out her breath, her lip quivering. She bites it hard, almost hard enough to draw blood, I'd bet.

"It's okay if you want to cry, you know," I tell her.

She shakes her head, pressing her teeth into her lip harder. "Momma said I can't cry. Only Oscar. I have to protect Oscar. I'm too big to cry."

"Oh, Sadie," I sigh. "Oscar will be okay for a few minutes. It's okay. I promise. Come here."

She finally breaks into tears, and the sobs rack her body so hard she's shaking and I'm hugging her to my chest and trying not to cry myself. She grabs hold of my shirt in tight fists and squeezes, bringing me as close to her as physically possible. I wonder miserably the last time someone's ever hugged her. I'd bet it wasn't recent.

"It's okay. It's okay."

I let her cry it out until she's quiet and rubbing at her eyes. I look at her and get her to take a few breaths with me because of how much that tends to help me out in my times of need.

"Are you gonna be okay?" I ask quietly.

Sadie nods like the big girl she is, sniffing hard and trying her best to collect herself. "Yes. I'll be okay. I'll see Mom again one day, won't I?"

"Of course," I reply, even though I have no idea. "You keep hope in your heart no matter what, and you'll see her."

She gives me a wobbly smile and then, grabbing her and Oscar's backpacks from atop her bed. She still has a few more things to put inside, so I go out into the living room to tell Gabriel she's getting ready to go.

I see Oscar, who's stopped crying and is holding Gabriel's hand.

"Oscar, Sadie's getting your backpack set. Do you want to go help her?"

He nods in his solemn way and heads down the hallway to meet his sister. I'm left alone with Gabriel, a man who I don't *really* know, but let's face it; they're all the same. They all have the same purpose to me and kids like me.

I approach him and try to look big and scary, crossing my arms and putting a scowl on my face. It's fear, fear for Sadie and Oscar and all the other kids just like them, that makes me say in my firmest voice, "Swear to me you'll never separate them."

Gabriel looks at me, confused. "What? I can't do that."

I shake my head once. "No. You don't understand. I don't care. They cannot be separated. They won't get on well without each other."

"Sweetheart, I can't tell you—"

"I don't want you to *tell me*. I want you to swear."

He still looks hesitant and confused, but he finally swears. I know it means virtually nothing, but I hope I've at least placed some doubt in his mind that separating them would be a good idea.

"I know I don't know you," I continue, "but don't *ever* call me sweetheart again, you creep."

I walk back to Sadie, feeling weirdly like myself, but also feeling bad for being rude to him. From someone who's met a decent amount of social workers, he doesn't seem like he's among the worst.

I see Oscar and Sadie out of the house and to the car that will take them to whatever's next for them. I feel an overwhelming sense of loss watching them go away in that car. I don't know what it is, but it kills something in my heart, and when I walk back up to Elizabeth where she stands in the doorway, I realize how messed up everything has become and feel the urge to break down.

With the exit of Sadie and Oscar, I now have to face my own life. No more distractions. No more ignoring it. That pain that's been festering inside of me for the past three days is rotting me from the inside out, and it hurts. It hurts really bad. And the longer I wait, the worse it will get. I know that. I just can't face it tonight.

When I get into bed to go to sleep, I listen for Sadie's breathing on the other side of the room. But I'll never hear it again.

CHAPTER TWENTY

The scorching hot, soapy water burns my fair skin as it runs down my hands into the sink. I scrub violently at the grimy pot with a Brillo pad, trying to get the hardened mashed potatoes off of it because I forgot to do it last night, like an idiot. Mostly I focus on the grounding of the pain as the boiling water hits my skin and steams, only so I don't have to focus on the pain in my brain that makes my negative thoughts spiral. What could've been, what *should've* been, all the things I hadn't considered because I put off my problems for Sadie's, yet another person in my life I've lost too quickly.

I thought I'd be more of a mess right now with the weight of my issues dropping back on my shoulders, but instead, it still doesn't feel real. Instead, it feels like the Kahales were something I dreamed up. Some part of me actually thinks there isn't any way I could've actually been somewhere so good, I could've *actually* messed up my chances at a real family. I sniffle suddenly, feeling my eyes line with tears I refuse to let fall.

A knock at the door makes me flinch, dropping the pot noisily into the sink. From her bedroom, Elizabeth asks if I can get the door. I hurriedly shut the sink off, drying my hands on my pants and walking to the door.

I open the door, my face blank, and barely even register who it is as I say, "Can I help you?"

"Lavender," says Jacob blankly.

I look up in surprise, confusion mangling my thoughts. I take in his disheveled appearance, from the tucked-in collar on his dress shirt, to the strand of hair that falls flat on his forehead. Even his eyes are a bit bloodshot, and I wonder if he's been working his ass off to get me out of here for whatever reason. Presumably, because he'd just love to see me in a group home for an eternity.

"Jacob? What are you doing here so soon? I thought I wasn't going to the group home for a few weeks," I say. I guess I could've missed a call from him, or maybe Elizabeth got one and forgot to tell me. I can't say I'm looking forward to this move, but it was inevitable.

But Jacob shakes his head. "No, no. That isn't why I'm here. It's the opposite, actually, I—"

"*Lavender!*" I hear, right before I am practically pummeled to the ground by someone tackling me.

The person's arms wrap around my stomach so tight I can't breathe, and when I look down, I smell the familiar scent of the Kahales' house—detergent and orange hand soap—and realize with a start it's Leia who's attached to my hip.

"Leia? Oh, my God, what are you doing here?" I ask, bewildered. My mind feels blank and speechless for once.

She's crying, and I'm afraid I might, too, and I'm so annoyed because I can't stop feeling like I'm going to cry, but I'm struck by the confusion again and I look back up at Jacob for an explanation.

My eye catches on something behind him though, and I cover my mouth with my hand so I don't throw up or cry or scream or something weird.

Elise, Drew, and Kai all walk to the front door, looking sorry and nervous but also happy. Really happy.

Leia detaches from me to look up at my face, and I absent-mindedly wipe her tears from her cheeks.

"Jacob, what is this? Why did you bring them here?" I inquire, trying to repress the rising feelings of joy that threaten to consume me. I can't let them before I know the full picture.

Elise chimes in from behind him. "We're here to pick you up."

I furrow my brow, pushing hair out of my face. "What? But I thought you sent me away. I thought you didn't want me anymore."

Elise shakes her head and comes to the doorway. Her smile is wobbly, eyes glossy. "That was never what happened. It was a misunderstanding, but it's all sorted out now. We've spent the weekend sorting it out so you could come back as soon as possible."

I'm still skeptical, so I look at Jacob for confirmation. He offers me a small but genuine smile. "The Kahales have decided to adopt you, Lavender. You'll be going home with them today. And every day after that, hopefully."

The news strikes me in my chest, and I feel the air leave my lungs. I can't do anything except look at all of them in disbelief, in utter amazement, because this cannot be real. This has to be a dream. It just has to.

"So?" Drew asks lightly, spreading his hands. "What do you think?"

I scoff, but my heart isn't in it. "What do I think? I think... hell yeah?"

Everyone laughs, but I still can't muster it. It isn't registering. I'm waiting for it to knock me over, to swallow me whole. But it's real. *It's real.*

"A-are you sure?" I ask breathlessly, which just earns me another wave of chuckles.

"We're sure, honey. Come here." Elise gestures for everyone to come, and I'm enveloped in a five-person hug I don't mind at all.

It's clumsy and filled with giggles and one "Ow, that's my foot, Kai!" from Leia, but it *is* happiness. I know this is the definition of happiness. I don't think I'd trade this moment for the whole world.

When we pull away, I notice there are a few tears in everybody's eyes, not just Leia's. But everyone also has huge smiles on their faces, and that is the confirming moment for me. This has always been real. It was never fake. The Kahales know what family means to them, and they've only just begun to teach me what it means. Already, I feel different. New.

Something's missing, though. And I realize it as I look at Kai.

"Can I ask... where's Emerson? Did you tell her about this?" I ask Kai directly, and everyone else looks away as if they don't want to talk about it. But not him.

Kai comes closer to me and I look up at him expectantly. He starts by saying, "Emerson isn't doing too well. I'm sorry."

"What? What happened to her?" I ask in a panic. My brain is still fogged and can't seem to comprehend any information, but my heart sinks warily.

But Kai shakes his head gently. "She's... she's actually in the hospital right now, unfortunately. She's okay. But it isn't my story to tell. I think you should hear it from her. She misses you."

Immediately I'm terrified, my negative thoughts taking over and forcing me to believe the worst. And as absolutely thrilled I am about the Kahales, worry fills my brain now. It's something about Emerson that has infiltrated me and will not go away, I'm sure. I know she feels it too, and I wonder how I will explain trying to cut her off.

"Can I see her today? When we get back?" I ask hopefully, looking to Elise and Drew.

They both nod and tell me Kai will take me once we're back.

"But for right now," Elise says, "it's time to get packed, all right?"

I nod, the smile coming back. And I head off to pack my bags again. This time, though, is my last.

* * *

Elizabeth is thrilled to have an empty home. I think I hear her muttering to Jacob about how she's done with foster children, but I try not to take it too personally.

The Kahales and I leave in Elise's car, Jacob in his own car, to wherever he has to go. The whole ride, everyone is asking me questions about the weekend to know about my experience with Elizabeth. I try to give the lightest, most surface-level responses I can so I don't get upset over it. My experience with Sadie was mostly emotionally-driven, and it was pretty much my entire experience at Elizabeth's house. I do mention Sadie, however, and the Kahales seem to like her from the way I describe. But, no offense, they'll never know how truly wonderful that kid is. I will, though, and I think that makes it sort of special.

We arrive back in Springfield around one o' clock in the afternoon, driving through the huge suburban houses, the cute little stores that line cobblestone streets. The sun is shining down on the town today, and people walk the streets in hoards, getting food, running errands. My eyes stay glued on them and I feel a sense of comfort knowing I am here to see them. I listen to Kai sing along to the radio and laugh when he asks me to join in, and even though I don't, I think Kai still knows how happy I feel inside. Weeks ago I was driving along this exact road, feeling hateful and ultimately dejected to have to experience yet another failed placement before the beginning of the end of my foster care experience truly commenced. It's almost comical how different I feel, how different I *am*. I bite my lip so I don't cry tears of joy as we pass by the diner.

When we pull into the driveway of the Kahales' home, we all pile out of the car. Everyone is in high spirits. I can tell they want me to come in and stay, but Elise encourages me to head straight to the hospital with Kai, so I hand her my backpack to take in and get right back in the car to head to Emerson.

On the way, I try to pry Kai for answers, but he doesn't give me very much. He tells me Emerson knows I'm being adopted, she'll live, and he can't tell me anything else. That doesn't stop me from trying, however, and by the time we get to the hospital, I know he's absolutely sick of me.

We head into the hospital and find Emerson's room with the help of a few secretaries and nurses. When we arrive at the room, I hesitate, nerves filling my veins. I'm scared of what I'll see in there. I hope she isn't in bad shape, and selfishly I hope she's not mad at me.

"I'm here if you need backup," Kai says from behind me.

I nod, brace myself, and walk inside.

Emerson lies in the bed wearing a standard hospital gown. She's paler than I've ever seen her. Her auburn hair lies on top of her head in that messy bun I love so much, with the little pieces framing her face. When she spots me, she looks so vulnerable my heart aches.

But her face lights up and a gasp leaves her mouth. "Lavender! Oh, my God, you're here!"

I smile and head over to hug her. Luckily, she smells not of hospital but of cinnamon and citrus. I pull away when the smell makes me feel so nostalgic I might break down right away.

"Hi, Emerson. It's good to see you," I say quietly. I offer her a small smile. I feel awkward, like this is our first time seeing each other, but she breaks that barrier down immediately.

"Come on, sit with me." She gestures for me to sit on the bed and scoots over a bit. I do so to face her fully. "I bet you have questions, huh?"

I nod. "Yeah, some. I bet you do, too."

She chuckles softly. "Some."

I decide to start so I don't have to focus on what I'm going to say while she's talking. "I only said what I said because I thought I'd never see you again. I didn't mean a word of it. I know it hurt, it hurt me too, and I'm sorry."

She looks down at her hands, a small smile on her lips, which I've noticed are chapped. "It's okay, Lavender. I get why you did it. I forgive you."

I let out a sigh of relief and relax my shoulders, feeling like at least one thing has been resolved.

After taking a deep breath herself, Emerson admits, "I had alcohol poisoning. I had to get my stomach pumped. I'm still here for observation. Or whatever, you know."

I furrow my brow. "Alcohol poisoning? Em, why did you drink that much?"

She looks at me curiously. "You called me Em. You never call me Em."

I look away, feeling embarrassed. "I'm sorry. I didn't mean to."

"No, no. It's okay. I like that." She's avoiding my question, I know, but gets serious when she sees the look on my face. "I don't know, Lavender, I just... I let it get out of hand. It won't happen again."

I let that sit for a few seconds, considering. I don't know if I'm being selfish by asking, but I ask anyway. "Emerson, is there any chance you got out of control because I wasn't around?"

She looks down at her hands again, fumbling around with the hospital blanket. "Yeah. Maybe. That could've been why."

Sighing deeply, I take one of Emerson's hands, forcing her to look up at me. "Look, remember when you told me this could be the start of something? Well, I know it felt like that for me too. But it can't happen like this."

Emerson looks at me and shakes her head, not understanding.

"I can't be your reason for living," I say forcefully. "You need to want to live for *you*. For Emerson. I'm not always going to be there to keep you sober, and then what? You'll lose control again? Is this what it was like before we met? You need to get help."

Emerson begins to cry almost immediately, and I feel terrible about it. But at the same time, I know she needs to hear this.

I soften my voice. "I'll be here for you. Always. But I want to see you be you. I want to see you prosper and have a life and really get to know yourself. I'll be there the whole time. But we can't be together until you want to live for *you*."

"I'll do better," Emerson says in a panicked voice, squeezing my hand. "I'll stop drinking. I can. I promise."

I shake my head. "You need to get better for *you*, Em. Okay?"

I can tell she's hesitating, but eventually, she nods. With that nod, I know there is an ending and a mutual understanding here. Not a goodbye. But still an end.

"I'll see you soon," I say, knowing in my heart it's right no matter how bad it hurts. But I don't say goodbye, because it would be too much.

Walking out of the room, I do not look back at her. I'm afraid seeing her cry will break my composure. So I walk into the hallway and right into Kai's arms.

CHAPTER TWENTY-ONE

Kai and I pull in the driveway after a silent car ride. I explained to him what happened and he told me I made the right choice. He assured me I would still see Emerson all the time but I set a healthy boundary and, at the same time, gave Emerson some motivation to work on herself.

He explained a little about Emerson before I arrived here but made it clear he didn't know much. She's always been in with the popular kids, who are notorious for their big parties filled with alcohol. He admits maybe Emerson had calmed down with the partying when I came around, even if she didn't stop completely. It makes me feel good, somehow, I brought out the best in Emerson. But it doesn't change my mind.

I promise myself I will text Emerson every single day, call her, drive to her house if I have to, to make sure she is doing okay. Though I can't be her lifeline, I want to be there for her. And I want her to be there for me, too. I think we both deserve as much.

I slam the car door shut with a sigh, my mixed feelings swirling around in my brain. Walking up to the front door with Kai, I let him open it for me and walk inside the warm house I've missed so much.

"*Surprise*!"

I look up and see Leia, Drew, and Elise all standing in the front hall, which they've decorated with lavender streamers and balloons. They've even made up a sign that says *WELCOME HOME, LAVENDER*! in huge, blocky, black letters.

I feel my hand cover my mouth to stifle my gasp and the following laughter. I'm surrounded on all sides by the Kahales as they come in for another family hug, which I accept with joy. In fact, I think I might *explode* from joy.

As they lead me to the kitchen where they've baked a purple cake with purple frosting messily done all around—which Leia proudly owns up to—I feel something I've never felt before. It's a combination of sheer happiness and something harsher, too, something that prods me in the chest and makes my throat ache with impending tears.

I'm still learning from the Kahales, yes. I don't think I'll ever stop learning from them. But it's them who got me here. All four of them. The love in their hearts and kindness they shower upon an undeserving world will never cease to amaze me. I mean, it worked on *me*. They transformed me from a sour-faced idiot with no trust in her heart to this mushy being I am today. And yes, it sounds embarrassing, but I don't care.

This is only the beginning of my journey with the Kahales. It won't always be perfect, and I know sometimes I'll hate it. In some ways, being the stoic foster child with trust issues was just easier. I didn't have to express myself or let people in or do any *work*. But that isn't what I wanted. *This* is what I want. A family. It's what I've always wanted. It's what everyone deserves, what Sadie and Oscar deserve instead of their mother who would dare choose drugs over them.

But even if it isn't with their biological mother in the end, it doesn't matter, because family can be found anywhere, in a number of different circumstances. Kai has his own little family in his friend group. Sadie and Oscar are each other's family. Every family is different, and not every family is blood-related.

I know that now. Because here I am, in *my* living room, in *my* home. With my family. And in this moment, as Kai smears purple frosting on my nose, I know this is where I've always belonged.

ACKNOWLEDGMENTS

Growing up as a book nerd whose biggest dream was to publish her very own book, I never thought the day would finally come when I did it. The journey was long, tedious, and mentally taxing, but the reward and gratitude I feel at this moment far surpasses any bumps in the road. Before entering this process, I did not quite understand the magnitude of publishing and owe my success to a boatload of people who made *Finding Lavender* possible. I wholeheartedly thank New Degree Press and all the extremely kind people who have been there for me from the start. I would also like to thank my whole family—Mom, Dad, Stephanie, and Mimi—for the unyielding support, for the genuine belief in me and my work that has only pushed me to do better and work harder. A great big thanks go out to my best friend Rebecca Gervitz. You have done nothing but cheer me on and I would never have been able to do this without you. Your feedback and love has gotten me where I am today, and I am so grateful. Thank you also to Ryan Hiemenz, the most helpful and thoughtful Beta Reader I could have ever asked for. *Finding Lavender* is only what it is today because of your help! Finally, there are so many people who single-handedly funded this publishing.

Your purchases of *Finding Lavender* have gotten me to this point, and I could not be more grateful. Therefore, I would like to thank the following people:

Jess & Nicole Abolafia

Nina Accardo

Stephanie Aguila

Demitrios Athanasoulis

Stephanie Arzu

Marie Bittman

Emma Birney

Zoey Blackman

Deborah Bonomo

Annie Burbage

Gabriella Cammarata

Misrraim Cardenas

Bonnie Cooper

Donna Croce

Debi Chozick

Kelly Culnan

Kory D'Angelo

Lia DiDonna

Jen Eagle-Baker

Anne Elluzzi

Camille Elluzzi

Dara Enny

Lee Esposito

Shari Esposito

Philene Evason-Bacon

Alexis Finley

Debi Fradkin

Kristin Goncalves

Stacy Greenberg

Katherine Harris

Susan Hart

Sarah Hashemi

Anna & Frank Hiliuk

Morgan Ivich

Shannon Jacobs

Maria Jimenez

Alexis Karlin

Eric Koester

Orly Krupkin

Zepha Leeking

Jayne Lieberman
Cristan Mariano
Melissa Mayol
Angelina Mendez
Deborah Mendez
John Mendez
Tonimarie Mendez
Christine Mott
Bashir Murtaza
Melissa Pescatore
Everett Phlipot
Judy Rothenberg
Samantha Savarese
Jordan Schlesinger
Lilly Shweky
Cheryl Soback
Rhonda Sorensen
Morgan Smith
Alexi Terris
Abby Thompson
Corinna Trapani
Nick Trapani
Sal Trapani
Lori Waldorf
Abby Worthington
Alyssa Wright
Suzanne Wycoff
Sandra Zeluck

APPENDIX

AUTHOR'S NOTE

"Overview of Findings (2018)." GLAAD, May 23, 2019. https://www.glaad.org/sri/2019/overview.

Winerman, Lea. "By the Numbers: LGBQ Teens Face Higher Suicide Risk." Monitor on Psychology. American Psychological Association, March 2018. https://www.apa.org/monitor/2018/03/numbers.

Printed in Great Britain
by Amazon

64996706R00136